STRATEGIC DESIGN

A Guide to Managing Concurrent Engineering

Practical "How To" Advice from America's Top Product Design Coach

Bart Huthwaite
The Institute for Competitive Design

Strategic Design: A Complete Guide to Managing Concurrent Engineering

Contents

ACKNOWLEDGMENTS i

FOREWORD iii

HOW TO READ THIS BOOK vi

Chapter 1.   What Concurrent Engineering Is And Why It Works 1

Chapter 2.   Your Greatest Hurdles And How To Overcome Them 13

Chapter 3.   Strategic Design: A New Method For
             Designing Blockbuster Products 19

Chapter 4.   The Twelve Principles Of Strategic Design 27

Chapter 5.   How To Start Your Concurrent Design Effort 39

Chapter 6.   Why You Must Use In-Process Measurements
             And Tools To Keep On Track 53

Chapter 7.   Maximizing Your Ilities:
             How To Build a Design Strategy 61

Chapter 8.   Reducing Product Complexity: Minimizing Your Ings 71

Chapter 9.   How To Measure Your Team's Efficiency 77

Chapter 10. How To Select Your Design Software With Less Pain 83

Chapter 11. Spreading The Word: How To Implement
             Concurrent Engineering Company-Wide 101

Chapter 12. How To Write Your Own Company User's Guide 111

Addendum   The Most Asked Questions About The Strategic
             Design Method 155

            Products and Services 158

Copyright 1994, Bart Huthwaite. Reproduction of any portion of this book is permittted for individual use if credit is given to Bart Huthwaite. Systematic or multiple reproduction or distribution of any part of this book or inclusion of material in publications for sale or internal company educational programs is permitted only with prior written permission or license.

Acknowledgments

During the past 11 years I have traveled over 3 million miles to more than 400 companies to coach over 1,000 product design teams. All I know about successful product design is the direct result of this hands-on experience.

The collective experience of these teams taught me the fundamentals which are at the core of my Strategic Design Method.

Space doesn't allow me to properly thank them all. But many of their companies are listed below.

Special thanks goes to ICD staff members Julie Hartz, Patricia Cook, Audrey Foley, and Bart Huthwaite, Jr. who through the years helped develop the concepts and material in this book.

Motorola	Allied-Garrett Engine Division
Caterpillar	FMC
ABB	Lockheed
Ericcson	Loral
Ford Motor Company	General Dynamics
Harris Corporation	TRW
3M	Bath Iron Works
Gulfstram Aerospace	Prince Corporation
Electrolux	Eaton Corporation
Hughes	Whirlpool
Storage Technology	Midmark Corporation
John Deere	General Electric
Rockwell International	Borg-Warner Automotive
Northrop	Smith Industries
Beckman Instruments	AEG Westinghouse

Dedication

To my wife, Nina,

who gave me the inspiration

to write this book.

Foreword

This is a "How To" book. It will give you step-by-step instruction in how to successfully manage a concurrent engineering design effort. No other book I know can do that.

It helps you take the mystery out of making concurrent engineering work by giving you a step-by-step design method developed over the past decade and validated at top corporations around the world. This methodology, which we call Strategic Design, will enable you to harness the full horsepower of your concurrent engineering team.

Strategic Design. This is not a rehash of Japanese design tools or management methods. It is based on my personal experience with more than 300 corporations and over 200,000 design team members I have had the pleasure of coaching since 1983.

Experience proves that three elements must be in place to have concurrent engineering work consistently. They are:

Methodology. Design teams need a new step-by-step way to harness the full power of their multi-functional effort. Most companies do not provide their design teams with a new design methodology. As a result, they fall back on what they have always done in the past with the same less-than-expected results.

This book gives you a new, proven concurrent engineering methodology to guide your team to success.

Measurement. Design teams need in-process measurement to know that their product design is on-track. They also need in-process measurement of their team efficiency. Most teams use few measurements and, in some cases, the wrong ones. Or they use post-process measurement, waiting until the product design is done before measuring how they have performed.

This book gives you tools for measuring in-process both your product design and your team efficiency, so that corrections can be made immediately.

Management. Design teams need management guidance and approval early in the product development. Without integrating management into the design process companies risk teams heading in the wrong direction with disasterous results.

This book gives you a way to integrate management into the design process without "turning off" the concurrent engineering team.

This is a hands-on book. You will be given new ideas, solid tools and proven instructions for designing new products faster, at lower cost and with better quality designed in.

You will be shown the secret of replicating a successful design process, how to repeat your winning design effort work with new teams, again and again.

This book is for you if you are championing the struggle to improve your design process as a:

- Manager
- Facilitator
- Team leader
- Team member

Too many of these champions suffer needless pain in their effort to overhaul their company's product development process. When they fail, as many do, they suffer loss of prestige and, yes, even their jobs. My book will keep you from suffering this same fate.

This book is for you if your:

- Senior management is demanding immediate results but doesn't really understand the real dimensions of your challenge.
- Department managers seem to be fighting you every step of the way.
- Team leaders are asking you for step-by-step instructions, methods and tools for guiding their team
- Team members are asking you to resolve the conflicts between their design team tasks and their functional department tasks.

What this book is *not*

This is not a book on teamanship. I strongly believe in the need for teamanship skills. But product designs mainly fail because of *poor design skills.* Strategic Design will show you how to strengthen your team's design skills.

This book is not a collection of Japanese design tools. I have used these tools and find them effective when applied at the right time, in the right way and by the right people. But the most effective design tools are those developed for the culture in which they will be used. Strategic Design is a book filled with design tools made in America for our uniquely creative environment.

This book is not another "design for manufacturability" handbook. I was a leader of the "design for manufacture and assembly" movement and wholeheartedly support any effort to reduce factory costs. But many times the greatest competitive advantage is not to be gained from "manufacturability." Strategic Design is a book that shows you how to design for all the "Ilities", especially the critical few that will make your team a winner.

The Strategic Design Method

Over the past years, I have learned the secrets of why some concurrent engineering teams fail and others win. I found that winning teams, most times unknowingly, solved their design problems in a unique, yet consistent manner. I began to construct a design method based on what I learned.

I trained other teams in my method, observing the results and then improving my tools and techniques further. This design methodology, which I now call Strategic Design, is based on what I have learned.

For many years I have resisted writing a book on my Strategic Design Method. My livelihood has come from giving on-site coaching and training in the technology of product design. For many years most of my clients requested that their successes with the Strategic Design Method not be published. They rightly viewed the techniques they learned as giving them a distinct competitive advantage.

But today more than 200,000 have been trained in the Strategic Design Method. It is being used around the world and is no longer considsered a secret weapon. This book represents the first time the method has been published.

How To Read This Book

Like all practical "How To" books, this one is designed to help you learn in a step-by-step manner. That's why you should not attempt to digest all of this book at one sitting.

First gain an **overall perspective** of concurrent design's real dimensions by reading **Chapters 1 and 2**. They will show you how to best **explain the process and its benefits** to your senior management and fellow employees, as well as the major hurdles awaiting you. The tips you learn from these chapters will pay valuable dividends and save you countless hours.

Then read **Chapters 3 and 4** to develop a solid **definition** and **operating principles**. You will discover that most of your fellow employees have quite different understandings. How you define the process will shape the outcome of your entire design effort.

Move to **Chapter 5** to learn about Strategic Design, a **step-by-step method for leading a concurrent design team**. This chapter will show you how to have your design team up to speed and on-track in only three days.

Then read **Chapters 6, 7 and 8**. These chapters give you new, **easy-to-learn** tools for harnessing your team's full horsepower. You will learn the key **rules for design tools**, how to **measure your design in-process**, how to **reduce time, improve quality** and **slash total cost**.

Move on to **Chapter 9** to learn how to **keep your team dynamics working well**. You will be given an easy-to-use tool to measure the health of your design team in-process.

Read **Chapter 10** for insight on the fundamentals of **selecting your computer design tools**. This chapter will save you untold grief as well as many thousands of dollars.

Spend time on **Chapter 11** if you are in charge of re-making your organization's design effort. This chapter gives you a concurrent engineering **implementation template** for rolling out concurrent engineering company-wide. This **step-by-step plan** helps you and your management understand what to do first.

Don't expect your company to grasp the "how to" of making concurrent design work without written guidance. **Chapter 12** gives you a proven technique as well as an already prepared **template for writing your own "Concurrent Design User's Guide."** Use this chapter to **customize your own version** to suit your company's needs.

The best of success to you. Please write me with any suggestions for future editions of this book. Or just pick up the telephone and call us at the Institute For Competitive Design. Our goal is to help you design winning products in any way we can.

>Bart Huthwaite
>The Institute For Competitive Design
>134 W. University Drive
>Suite 307
>Rochester, Michigan 48307
>Phone: 313-656-2195
>Fax: 313-656-2365

Chapter 1.

What Concurrent Engineering Is And Why It Works.

It's Monday morning and the boss calls you with a request. "Our design process," he says, "just isn't working. What we need is an overhaul, well beyond what we've ever done in the past."

You listen carefully, a sense of foreboding already creeping into your mind. "Go out and find the best way to fix it," the boss continues.

Now you are really concerned. You remember Charlie, who had the job of introducing the last "program of the month." And then there was Joe, who tried to launch something called "simultaneous engineering" several years back.

Both of these guys are no longer with your company.

You energetically agree to "do my best" and begin what is to become one of the most frustrating assignments in your entire life.

It's now three months since that fateful phone call. The boss is still waiting for "positive results." And you are still struggling with the step-by-step "how to" of meeting his request.

It's not that you haven't tried. You've benchmarked other companies. You have several concurrent engineering conferences under your belt. And a stack of new books on the subject are scattered across your desk.

But nowhere have you found the "rubber hits the road," step-by-step "how to" your are seeking.

Sound familiar? Don't feel alone. Join the crowd.

Almost all the concurrent engineering champions I meet are frustrated by the lack of step-by-step instruction in how to make the process really work in their company.

That's why I have written this book. It will give you a map, tools and, most important, measurements for making you successful at your difficult task.

In this first chapter you will learn the first step in laying the groundwork for a successful implementation effort. How well you complete this first step will be a major factor in shaping your final results.

Your first task:

Clearly communicate the real dimensions of concurrent engineering.

You will find most in your company do not really understand how tough it is to make it work well. And most will have widely different views on how to define the process.

Many will see it as just another engineering tool. Others will understand it means a major change to your product delivery process.

But few, at first, will clearly grasp the real truth:

Reshaping your design process requires a fundamental change in your organization's culture.

Your first all-important task is to educate your company in this fact and what it really takes to make it "part of the woodwork."

The first people you must educate are your senior managers. They are the group which will have to fund and continually support this cultural change. Without them, you are at a high risk of failure.

Here are the 9 most important facts you must know and be able to communicate effectively. Your most effective way will be to present the following in a 30-45 minute overview presentation.

I include an example to support each fact. You may wish to add your own personal observations from your company's recent history.

1. Design influences more than we think.

How we design a product determines 70% — or more — of its life-cycle cost, quality and cycle time. Most people in your company may not realize this fact.

You must drive this fact home in every presentation you make. We generally spend too much time, too late, and in the wrong place "fixing" our product problems.

Billions were spent in the past decade on the factory floor attempting to improve quality and cost.

In reality, much of this was wasted. The factory floor was merely the "symptom," or effect, of the real culprit. Manufacturing processes are determined by how we design. Trying to change or improve them on the factory floor is like shutting the barn door after all the horses are out.

Example: The quality improvement movement in America began on the factory floor. Tools such as statistical process control (SPC) were introduced to better understand and control manufacturing processes. These techniques have yielded far better quality.

Yet companies today are awakening to the realization that world class quality is determined by the kind of manufacturing processes we select at the early design stage.

The real "fix" for a bad manufacturing process is not more control on the factory floor but the elimination, or simplification, of that process at the early design stage.

2. We are great at innovation, but poor at implementation.

We in the Western World lead in product innovation. Yet too often we fail to reap the benefits of our new technology.

Our biggest problem is product delivery, the task of transitioning our innovation to commercial success. We don't spend enough time early enough working on the "how to" problems of commercializing our technical success.

You must show how concurrent design, properly understood and applied, can cure this flaw. It brings together at the "front end" of the design effort all those who must eventually implement the tasks, or processes, a design sets in motion.

These process owners are the key to making sure all the commercial pitfalls are covered.

Example: Remind your listeners that every Fall newspapers herald the Nobel Science Prize winners. The Western World consistently dominates the list for scientific innovation.

Pacific Rim nations are far down the list. Yet turn to the business pages in the same paper and you'll find they are leading the technical commercialization race.

Tell them concurrent design can be used to improve both commercialization as well as innovation.

3. We squander design horsepower.

We don't leverage the power of design enough. You must point out that your organization's design process is an untapped resource.

For example, most design teams don't reach far enough in reducing total product life cycle cost. Most focus on the "direct," highly visible and documented costs of labor and material used on the factory floor.

Very few design teams attack your company's greatest cost challenge: indirect costs. These are everything other than labor and material. They include such overhead expenses as supervision, material storage, rework, as well as hundreds of other expenses.

Your accounting department collects these costs under the heading of "overhead" or "burden." These "pooled" costs are then tacked on to direct labor, or material, as a "labor/burden" factor. Every dollar of direct labor cost, for example, then carries with it this additional "burden" cost. Such costs can be 4-6 times more than the direct labor cost.

Such costs can account for over 30% of a total product's manufactured cost. Design cannot eliminate all indirect costs. And all indirect costs are not "bad."

But few design teams are very educated in how to reduce these kinds of costs. Fewer still are ever challenged by management to attack them at the design stage.

Most think these indirect "hidden" costs can only be attacked at the "symptom," factory floor level and not at the design, or "causal" level.

Example: Challenge your audience to try this simple design-for-cost test. Have them ask a design team to show them how their new design will reduce the direct costs of labor and material expense.

They can usually show how they have reduced part count to reduce labor. And they can usually point to material cost reductions.

But then ask them to show you how they have reduced indirect, or "overhead" expenses. Chances are they will give you a blank stare. Or they may even say "those aren't our job...that's management's job on the factory floor."

Most concurrent engineering teams are not trained or motivated to make indirect cost part of their design equation, despite the fact that the design stage is the best place to begin attacking it.

The chapters which follow will clearly show you how to train and motivate design teams to reduce these indirect costs.

4. We must have a larger view of "product."

Most of your designers think of "product" as a series of parts. And many of them have received excellent training in reducing the cost of these parts.

You may even have given training in "design-for-manufacture and assembly."

But a "product" is far more than a series of parts.

A product is the sum of the life cycle steps required to design, manufacture, field support, and, finally, dispose of it.

This is a "systems" view of product design. Your challenge is to widen the design perspective of your company. You must free them from the notion that design is only for engineers working on the drawing board or factory floor.

You must show them that in order to understand these life cycle implementation tasks, *design is everybody's job.*

Example: In the late eighties, many companies launched efforts to reduce product part counts. The idea was that fewer parts meant less manufacturing and assembly cost.

Many of these part reduction efforts yielded major cost reductions. But too many ended in failure. What happened? In their rush to reduce parts, mainly by combining several parts into one, designers moved away from standard, off-the-shelf, high-volume parts.

Many new designs also led to complex tooling and longer lead times. And many designs even ignored ease of service in favor of better "manufacturability."

You must educate them in the fact that all Ilities must be reviewed at the early design stage, not just manufacturability.

5. Concurrent engineering is not "new."

Never describe concurrent engineering as something "new." It has been around for decades and will still be used in years to come.

Many smaller companies practice its principles today without even calling them "concurrent engineering."

But with larger companies, producing highly technical products, the challenge is far greater. Many developed specialized functional departments through the years to deal with the increasing complexity of their growing product lines.

These departments had their own budgets, personnel, and points of view. Too often this resulted in a breakdown in communication between departments. Many even began to narrow their focus to only their departmental goals, ignoring their company-wide goals.

Today these companies are simply "returning to their roots." They are re-discovering the basic fundamentals which made them a success in their early years.

Example: Share with your company the Ford Taurus story. Ford engineers launched their Taurus design effort using what they called "simultaneous engineering." All car engineering groups were gathered together at the early design stage to try and slash development time.

Their success made trade paper headlines with many describing the process as a "new engineering technology." As a Ford engineering manager laughed, "Henry Ford would probably roll over in his grave if he read that headline. That's the way Ford developed the Model T!"

6. There is no "one size fits all."

Beware of "silver bullet" cure-all solutions. There is no single "cookbook" answer for rebuilding your product delivery process.

Each company has a different product design culture. What may work well in a smaller, tightly-knit company may be a total failure in a larger, more bureaucratic organization.

Design challenges also differ. What may work for one product design effort within a company may not work for another.

You must shape your implementation effort to fit both your culture and the kind of design challenge you are facing. Communicate this right from the start to both your senior managers and team members. You will save yourself much grief later.

There are however, some basic fundamentals. These are spelled out in Chapters 11 and 12.

But the first, and most basic one, is that the people who must implement your concurrent engineering effort — that is, make it work — are the ones who should have a hand in designing its implementation.

Teach them the fundamentals and then let them shape the process to "fit" your company culture. They are the ones who know it best. And they are the ones who must implement the process in the final analysis.

Example: Write your own "in-house" concurrent engineering "User's Guide" and include a section answering "how to" questions asked by your own people and answered by them.

This builds the ownership of the process. It also gets the tough questions surfaced right away. Chapter 12 will show you how to do this.

7. There is no "quick fix."

Too many managers don't really understand the difficulty you face. Educate them fast. If you don't, you are headed for trouble. As one project leader once said "It ain't something we are going to fix overnight."

Culture changes take time. Your design culture has been built over years. Many managers in your company may even feel "If it isn't broke, why fix it?"

Yet too many managers want the "quick fix." They tire quickly over the long haul.

Other managers see concurrent engineering as a "tool" that need only be taught and immediately change will happen. Set them straight right away.

This kind of narrow thinking can be extremely dangerous for your career.

Example: The product development improvement effort in the United States has gone through two phases and we are now into our third.

The first phase was a fascination with design tools. The idea was that we were simply using the "wrong" tools. All we had to do was add some new ones and all would be well.

Thousands were taught in such techniques as Design of Experiments, Design for Assembly, Design for Manufacturability, Quality Function Deployment and other design tools. There were some success stories. But consistent, day-in and day-out success was hard to find.

The second phase was the "simultaneous engineering" or concurrent engineering era. This is the one the United States is in now. The problem is that our product development process is broken, you will hear many argue.

The reason why the tools brought no lasting success, is that they could not be *integrated* into the product development process. Multi-functional design teams were formed and even co-located but consistent success still eludes most companies.

Only now are we seeing that the entire company culture must be supportive. We are finally recognizing that changing the design process impacts everyone. The entire company must share in the change process if we are to see repeated success.

Smart managers recognize this. They reverse the historical process by first clearly stating the philosophy that *design is everybody's job*.

They then support a change in the design process itself, encouraging those who will use the new process to shape it to fit their own needs. Smart managers also realize that design is as much a social challenge as it is a technical challenge.

And they leave the choice of what tools to use up to the design teams who must use them. These "users" know best what tools to use and when.

8. We have poor design skills.

I have coached thousands of concurrent engineering teams and find that, with only few exceptions, most have poor design skills. But why should they?

Most members on a multi-functional design team have never been called upon to participate in the design creation process before. Their on-the-job training is nil.

I also find, however, that many who are titled "product designer" have poor design skills. They may have very good engineering skills, but there is a wide gulf between "engineering" skill and "design" skill.

Engineering skill is taking a technical problem with a set of requirements and working these to reach an optimum solution.

Design skill is first asking "are we working on the right problem, in the right way and at the right time?" Design skill is the ability to find new problems to solve, well beyond a customer's "requirements."

Design skill is the ability to wrestle with technical, social, and business issues simultaneously and reach an optimum solution for both the customer and his company.

Example: The first question I ask a new client is "Are you practicing concurrent engineering now?" The answer almost always comes back as a resounding "Yes!"

When I probe a little deeper and ask "What are you doing?," the response is usually "We have formed multi-functional teams, trained them in team-building and co-located them."

But when I ask "What else?" the response is usually a blank stare.

Successful teams need coaching, training and practice to make them winners. The All-Star U.S. Basketball team in the recent Olympic games received rigorous coaching, training, and practice. Under skillful coaching, they developed their own unique method of play and then perfected it through weeks of training and practice.

You must do the same thing. Chapters 3-5 give you a technique for doing this.

9. Needed: A new design methodology.

Old methods yield old results. Just because you assemble a multi-functional design team, co-locate them, and then train them in team building doesn't guarantee you a thing.

In fact, many on your team will continue to play the same, limited role in the design process they have before.

Manufacturing team members will wait for the product designers to complete the design for their "review." Meanwhile, product designers will grouse about the "lack of input" from the manufacturing people.

You must give your concurrent engineering team a new design method if you are to expect new results.

Example: The Strategic Design method, described in Chapter 5 of this book, was developed over the past decade to harness the full horsepower of a concurrent engineering team. It gives your design teams a series of step-by-step tasks to make sure they are headed in the right direction and, at the same time, have the buy-in of their management.

Strategic Design gives the team *in-process* measurements for rating how well their design effort is meeting their goals.

Its success is based on that fact that without such a step-by-step method, coupled with in-process measurement, too many design teams waste time, dollars, and opportunity. The bottom line result: flawed products.

A New Definition For Design

It should be quite clear now that you must give management and everyone in your company a new perspective on "design," a new, wider definition for this process. Here is the one I use:

The process of integrating all the commercial, as well as technical, attributes required by a competitive product during its entire life span.

This definition carries "design" well beyond just meeting a product's technical requirements. It emphasizes that design directly impacts commercial success and that everyone who must help implement a product design must be part of the design creation process.

It clearly says that **design is everybody's job.**

Chapter Summary

In this chapter, you learned how to communicate the real dimensions of concurrent engineering to management and your fellow design team members. You now have a new definition for "product design" which recognizes that product development is "everybody's job."

You now have the 10 key points you need to convince others that their help is essential for gaining the benefits of concurrent design.

In the next chapter, you will learn the major hurdles awaiting you as you begin to apply concurrent engineering techniques and how to overcome them.

Chapter 2.

Your Greatest Hurdles And How To Overcome Them

Contrary to what you read in the industrial press, most companies still have yet to master the ability to consistently bring products to market at the right time, at the right price, and with the right customer needs fulfilled.

Why do so many product design efforts still flounder? We at the Institute for Competitive Design sought the answer from those who know best: design team leaders, corporate managers, and others who are directly responsible for making the design process work.

Knowing these answers will help you learn from their mistakes as well as better prepare you for your task.

Here are your ten greatest hurdles. Following each are brief notes on proven solutions, or "cures."

Slow Start

The downstream process owners, those who must implement the product design, are not involved early enough. The design team is first staffed by the "technology experts" with all other Ilities joining the team after the start-up phase.

The result: a lack of total design ownership and constant bickering. All too often the "latecomers" end up calling their team member's "baby" ugly. Also costly, time-consuming engineering changes emerge as new issues, not anticipated by the original team members, surface later in the design cycle.

The Cure: Encourage pro-active involvement of all the process owners, or Ilities, from Day One. Encourage these downstream process owners to educate the functional design experts on their previous, all too painful design flaws.

Require a well-disciplined, frank discussion on the enterprise-wide business problem, from the standpoint of all the Ilities so that there is total agreement on the global design problem before anyone begins to solve it.

No Methodology

There is no disciplined methodology, or "road map," to guide design teams. No step-by-step system for analyzing customer benefits, and exploring all the Ilities is in place. Multi-functional teams are formed, but no system is used to integrate all Ility issues, or complete the necessary design "trade-offs." Design teams squander the most important design stage: the concept stage. With impending deadlines, teams are forced to agree on the most convenient solution.

The Cure: Use a design method to explore design problems, develop a competitive strategy, and develop innovative solutions. Adopt a formal procedure to integrate all Ilities early enough to impact design solution.

Few In-Process Measurements

Management uses traditional metrics of performance, such as simply a time schedule and direct cost to measure team success. Little attention is given to measuring a product's serviceability, indirect cost, and other factors beginning early in the design cycle. Opportunities are missed for improving these product features.

The Cure: Educate teams in how to measure all Ilities right from the start of their design. Ask them to measure those which will do the greatest good for total product competitiveness. Encourage management to set the broad product goals, allowing the design team to set the intermediate goals. This builds team understanding and buy-in. Make sure teams understand their goals must be subjected to management review and approval.

Poor Team Efficiency

Teams begin designing their product without designing their organizational process first. Roles for each team member are unclear. How decisions are to be made is uncertain. The authority of the team leader is in question. Timetables are missed as poor human dynamics block organizational efficiency. Decisions are not carried out, or even supported, due to poor buy-in.

The Cure: Design your organizational process first, your product design second. Begin with your decision-making process. Decide up front how and who will make what kinds of decisions. Recognize that a decision which cannot be implemented is worthless. Focus on both the quality of the decision and the quality of the implementation.

Wrong Tools

Design teams use the wrong tools, in the wrong way, at the wrong time. For example, a design team uses a design-for-manufacturability tool to reduce factory cost. Only later do they discover their design is more manufacturable but is almost impossible to service. Another team uses QFD (Quality Function Deployment) to fine-tune a product to a particular customer's needs, only finding out later that another potential market was completely missed. In another case, hundreds of employees are trained in design-of-experiments (DOE) which they never use and may be eventually forgotten.

The Cure: The product team must first define their design problem and then select the correct tools to solve it. Training in design tools is best done immediately before they have to use them. All team members should be trained in the tools eventually selected.

Management Inaction

Management does not have a model for their meaningful participation in the product development process. Management fails to interact with the design team in a pro-active way. Any interaction which does occur is in a review manner, usually late in the design cycle. Conflicts between the team's design and management's goals are discovered and must be fixed at great expense and loss of team morale.

The Cure: Integrate management into the design cycle right from the start. Have management review and coach the team, step-by-step, as it first defines the design problems, develops a design strategy and then begins the process of innovation. Such an incremental approach catches misunderstandings early in the design cycle, when they can be fixed at minimum cost.

Limited Perspective

The product design team fails to see the big picture. They define their design boundaries too narrowly. Design teams fail to see their product as a system of process steps, instead concentrating on reducing factory part count and cost. Opportunities for reducing design cycle time, and customer product integration cost are lost.

The Cure: Educate teams in global process design, the skill of understanding a product's potential for creating total life cycle process steps. Measure designs by how they reduce global process complexity, not just reduce factory parts.

No "How To" Guidelines

Design teams are unclear about the "How to" of concurrent product development. Teams lack a User's Guide to help them solve organizational and other problems. No documentation is in place to learn from previous company design failures and successes, hence, the team is unable to benefit from lessons learned.

The Cure: Develop your own company-specific Concurrent Design User's Guide. Ask those who must make concurrent design work to help write it. Poll design team members for questions and then use your User's Guide as a tool for answering them company-wide. Include stories about previous company successes — and failures. Capture examples of future design success in your User's Guide as they occur.

Poor Cost Understanding

Design teams fail to understand cost, especially indirect cost, and how it can be reduced at the early design stage. They have little knowledge about total life cycle product cost. Design teams focus on internal direct cost, ignoring indirect costs such as inventory, re-work, overhead, and other myriads of hidden costs created by a product design. Worse, teams reduce internal visible costs but create high integration cost for the customer. Design teams attack cost problems that the accounting department can count best, but which may not be the biggest cost reduction opportunity. Direct costs shrink but indirect, overhead costs soar.

The Cure: Move beyond conventional, internal accounting procedures to attack all costs, both internal and external. Educate design teams in how their designs create indirect expense, including hidden overhead costs. Integrate customer costs directly into design equation.

Lack of Practice

Team begins design task cold. Little warm up time is allowed for understanding problems with existing designs.

The Cure: Have team practice on improving another existing design before launching their design effort. This gives them the opportunity to understand their problem, as well as themselves, better.

Chapter Summary

In this chapter, you learned the major hurdles facing a concurrent engineering effort and cures for overcoming them. Understanding these hurdles allows you to prepare for them. The result is that there will be fewer unexpected surprises facing you.

In the next chapter you will learn a step-by-step method for building a solid foundation for your design effort. This new methodology will help you get your design effort right from the start.

Chapter 3.

Strategic Design: A New Method For Designing Blockbuster Products

It should be clear by now that changing your company's product design process is not an easy task. Implementing concurrent engineering is vastly different than tweaking your product delivery process.

But what, exactly, must you do to be a success? What are the step-by-step actions you must take to make both you and your company a winner?

Unfortunately, it's impossible for me to give you a "one-size-fits-all" answer. Your company, like all others, has its own unique products, markets and culture. You must customize your implementation plan to fit your own company.

But what I can do is give you fundamentals, "must do" steps and tools I have developed over the past 12 years to make concurrent engineering really work. The proof of their value is the fact they are now being used by more than 200,000 engineers and thousands of design teams at successful companies worldwide.

I have combined these into what we now call the Strategic Design Method. When someone asks me for a quick definition I simply answer **"Designing a product as a system for lower cost, better quality and less time."**

The word *system* is key. Strategic Design *doesn't* mean focusing on one specific design issue, such as manufacturability. It means analyzing *all the Ilities* and deciding which ones are really important for success. Strategic Design addresses the *total business problem*, not just the technical design problem.

Here is a more complete definition:

> Stategic Design is a step-by-step, customer-focused, team-centered, technology for reducing cost, improving quality, and shrinking cycle time by simplifying a product's system of life cycle tasks at its early design concept stage.

Strategic Design meets the eight requirements essential for a concurrent engineering effort to be successful:

1. Requirement: "Step-by-step"

Concurrent engineering is radically new to most design teams. Design teams need guidance in moving from their old sequential over-the-wall approach to the newer way of concurrent engineering. Both you and senior management must give them a game plan for making sure they have covered all the bases. Don't expect them to invent one for themselves.

Strategic Design sets out a five-step "Road Map" for making sure your design team is concurrently focusing on the right design issues, in the right way and at the right time. It pulls together all the needs of the team members, enabling them to quickly reach consensus on a winning design strategy. Strategic Design also brings you and senior management into the loop to make sure that all are in agreement, every step of the way.

2. Requirement: "Customer focused"

Strategic Design focuses attention on exceeding customer requirements. It challenges your design team to go well beyond requirements and search for ways to bring the customer benefits he is not even expecting.

For example, it defines cost as "the total cost of ownership," not the purchased price of the product. Strategic Design shows your team how to build a cause and results relationship between the product that will eventually be shipped to the customer and the features of its design.

It ranks the customer Ilities of functionality, installability, serviceability and others higher, for example, than your internal Ilities of manufacturability and assembleability. But at the same time, Strategic Design requires your design team to balance their customer needs against your own company needs.

3. Requirement: "Team-centered"

Design implementation, not technical innovation, is the biggest stumbling block manufacturers face today. We are the leaders in world technology but somehow we lose when it comes to delivering the goods faster, with better quality, and at lower cost.

Strategic Design integrates the design implementation needs of all the process holders from the early conceptual stage of the design effort. For example, the "voice" of the Service Department is heard as well as the "voice" of the Customer. The understanding and support of these process owners is needed for fast, effective implementation. The goal is total buy-in and ownership up front in the early design stage.

All the tools, techniques and measurements used with the Strategic Design Method are team-centered. That is, they are impossible to be used without the input and buy-in of your entire design team.

4. Requirement: "Reduce cost"

Sadly, few design teams really understand how to design for total cost reduction. This is not their fault. Our accounting systems are ineffective for predicting both a product's *total shipped cost* as well as *life cycle* cost. Life cycle cost includes the cost of servicing and disposing of a product. These costs are simply beyond the scope of your internal accounting system.

But design teams are also not very skilled at reducing total shipped cost. These are *all your internal costs of developing, manufacturing, and administering a product.* Your accounting system does do a good job of capturing direct product costs such as labor and material. But more than 30% of all product cost is pooled as indirect cost and is not given to your design team in any meaningful way. This indirect cost is hidden from the view of your design team and usually ignored in their design equation.

Strategic Design considers this hidden cost as the real cost battleground today. It gives your design team tools for identifying and reducing such indirect expense, beginning at the early design stage. It enables them to make hidden cost part of their design equation.

5. Requirement: "Improve quality"

Quality begins with design. While the factory floor quality revolution has yielded astounding results, only by designing a product for quality production can these results be sustained.

Product quality begins with your design team clearly understanding the difference between manufacturing processes which can consistently yield quality results and those which are constantly creating quality problems. You must make design for quality a part of the design equation, right from the beginning.

Strategic Design enables your design to solve quality problems at the early design stage. Strategic Design does this by giving them tools for analyzing potential quality problems, helping them find solutions, and giving them a yardstick for measuring the results.

6. Requirement: "Shrink cycle time"

Slashing time-to-market is now recognized as a key factor in gaining competitive advantage. Short cycle product development carries with it three major benefits. The first benefit is that a product's sales life is extended. For each month cut from a product's development cycle, a month is added to its sales life. Shrinking development time also frees up valuable engineering time for other product introductions.

The second benefit is increased market share. The first product to market has a 100 percent share of the market in the beginning. The earlier a product appears, the better are its prospects for obtaining and retaining a larger share of the market.

The third benefit is higher profit margins. The first company to market typically enjoys more pricing freedom.

You must be able to give your design team coaching, training and a method for significantly reducing their design time without degrading the quality of their design. Strategic Design will help you do this because it reduces *the complexity of the design process.* In addition, it gives your design team a method for coping with the human dynamics of making design decisions.

7. Requirement: "Simplify a product's system of life cycle tasks"

You must coach your design teams to see "product" as far more than merely a set of functional requirements which finally result in an assembly of manufactured parts. A product is really a series of interrelated tasks, initially set in motion by design, which only end when that product is finally disposed of at the end of its useful life cycle.

This is a *systems* view of a product. Most design teams focus too intently on meeting functional needs and reducing manufactured part costs. Indeed, management encourages them to think this way by using these two factors as their key measurement yardsticks. Yet the greatest opportunity for product improvement lies in seeing "product" in a larger scale, as a series of life cycle business tasks.

Help your design team understand this big picture and you will be astounded by the results. For example, a West Coast electronics components manufacturer struggled unsuccessfully to gain a cost edge over its major competitor. Every cost reduction it was able to achieve was met by an equal cost reduction by its competitor. Then, one of their design teams proposed designing component packaging to better protect shipped parts, yet also reduce their customer's unpacking and waste disposal costs. The customer immediately saw the benefits on his factory floor in time, quality assurance, and cost. Meanwhile, the competitor no longer could simply slash component cost to compete. The design team had "changed the rules of the game." It saw "product" as more than the sum of component's manufactured cost.

Strategic Design gives your design team tools to map the total processes required by their design solutions. This enables them to spot potentially complex business processes. It also pinpoints the processes which will create the biggest problems later in the product's life span.

This systems view is in keeping with the movement today toward "reengineering," the task of rethinking and simplifying business processes. The power of Strategic Design is that it helps your design team "reengineer by design." That is, solve the business process problem before it ever reaches the floor.

Institute for Competitive Design

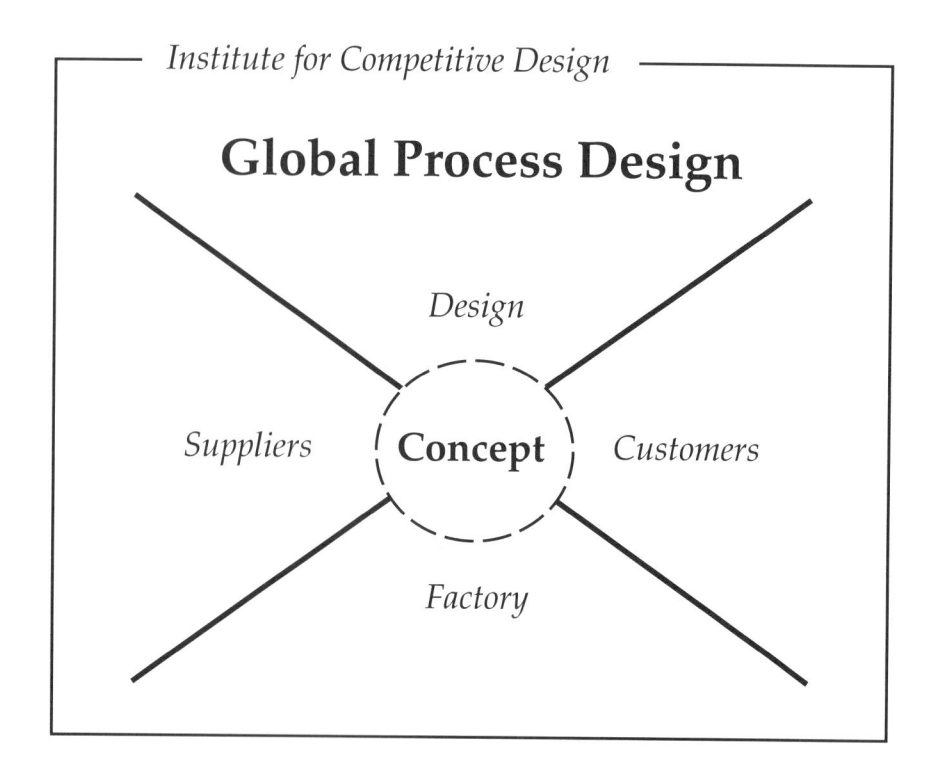

Global Process Design

Design

Suppliers **Concept** *Customers*

Factory

8. Requirement: "Begin at the early design concept stage"

The concept stage of your design effort "drives" 70% — or more — of your eventual cost, quality, and time-to-market. By "concept," I mean all that a design team does until it begins to "detail" the individual parts in their design. Once your team commits to parts, they have left the "systems" stage of their effort.

Too many teams leave this first stage of design with flawed concepts. The price they pay is the cost, in time and dollars, for seemingly endless design changes, trying to correct later what they could have "fixed" for little or nothing in the early design phase.

Why do they leave so soon? One reason is the lack of a step-by-step methodology to guide them through this fertile phase. The design team quits the "thinking" phase too soon, rushing to the "task" phases of part detailing and prototyping where they can "see the result" of their work.

But management is also a culprit. Having no way to measure the quality of what the team is doing in the concept stage and not being a part of the process, management nudges the team into the "hard lines" stage in order to "see some results."

Yet management cannot be blamed too much. Many times design teams have asked for more time up front, at the concept stage, yet the results are still the same — delayed product launches. What happened? Close review usually shows that the design team *did not change their method of design.* They used their old tools and got what could be expected — old results.

Strategic Design gives your design team a new method for making concurrent engineering work. It requires your entire team to be "in place" and working as a team at the concept stage. Strategic Design gives them a solid, step-by-step method for heading in the right direction. And, at the same time, it gives you and your management both a voice in the process as well as measurement tools for tracking results.

Chapter Summary

In this chapter, you learned why applying the Strategic Design method can yield blockbuster products in shorter time and with less cost. Most concurrent design teams fall far short of their expectations because they do not fundamentally change how they design. They use old methods and get old results.

Strategic Design gives your team a new way of thinking about product design. It busts old paradigms about design and helps every member of the team clearly see their new role. Strategic Design harnesses the full horsepower of your concurrent engineering effort.

In the next chapter you will go "back to basics" and learn a set of 12 design principles needed to achieve product excellence. These are at the core of the Strategic Design method.

Chapter 4.

The Twelve Principles Of Strategic Design

Today competitive design requires a radical new way of thinking.

Failure to change the way you think about designing products today can mean annihilation for you tomorrow. Many companies are already developing products in half the time required just five years ago. Most are doing this with fewer resources, better quality, and far lower product costs. Just how can they do this?

These companies are able to reach these goals because they have adopted a radically different view of "product design." They see the product development in a far different way than most. These innovative organizations have a new, far broader definition for the word "design." They believe that:

> Design is the strategic integration of all product life cycle goals at the early concept stage.

The Strategic Design Method has been developed to facilitate this objective. Strategic Design is a methodology based on the reality that what we describe as "product" is really a system of complex process steps which are set in motion at the product's innovation stage and do not end until the product's final disposal.

Strategic Design requires that all the "owners" of these complex process steps be actively involved in creating the product design, in order that their needs are part of the total design equation. Product design is far more than identifying and integrating a product's technical requirements. It is seeking, defining, solving, and integrating a product's *total business requirements*.

Strategic Design integrates these product life cycle goals at the "front end" of the design effort, where the cost of integration is low and the leverage high.

In the past, many companies formed multi-functional concurrent engineering teams hoping to design for these total business requirements.

Too often, the result was disappointing. The reason: The team lacked *(1) a step-by-step methodology, (2) easy-to-use tools, and (3) measurements to guide them to success.*

The Strategic Design Method fills this gap. It gives your design team a "road map" to guide them during the critical first 24 working hours of a design effort. It teaches them easy-to-learn tools to help them design better. And it shows them how to measure their design while they are actually creating it.

Strategic Design is used for a new product or an existing one. It can be used throughout the design effort or just at the start. And it does not replace any existing design delivery process you have in place.

Nor does it defeat the purpose of other design tools such as Quality Function Deployment (QFD), Design of Experiments (DOE), Design for Manufacturability and Assembly (DFMA). The Strategic Design Method is usually used before these design tools.

Chapter 5 will give you instruction in how this powerful methodology works. But first you must understand its underlying philosophy.

Following are the 12 basic principles of the Strategic Design Method. Today they are being used throughout the world to design products ranging from cellular telephones to appliances, from the Space Shuttle to kitchen sinks, and from microchips to potato chips.

The Strategic Design Method applies equally to a product as well as to a service. These 12 principles must be clearly understood and applied by your design teams. They must be at the *core of your competitive design effort* if you are truly to attain your key goals of better quality, lower price and faster delivery.

In order to challenge conventional design thinking, many years ago I invented new words to communicate these new ideas.

Following is this new lexicon:

"Life Cycle" – The time span between the creation of a product idea to its final disposal as a product at the end of its life.

"Ility" – A positive product attribute, i.e.., serviceability, manufacturability, marketability, etc.

"Ing" – Any task required to create, design, manufacture, service, or dispose of a product, i.e.., documenting, machining, installing, re-cycling, etc.

"Visible Ings" – Product processes and tasks easily recognized by a design team and well-tracked by conventional accounting methods. Examples are manufacturing processes such as machining, molding, etc.

"Hidden Ings" – Product tasks not captured by traditional accounting methods in any way meaningful for a product design team, i.e.., indirect corporate expenses such as "overhead" and "fixed" costs, marketing, inventorying, purchasing, and other indirect costs.

"Ing Owner" – A person responsible for performing an Ing anywhere in the product's life cycle. Ing Owners are experts at understanding how Visible Ings create the need for Hidden Ings.

"Things" – Combinations of both hidden and visible Ings i.e.., a product and its integrated parts and processes, both visible and hidden. "Things" are best understood as "bundles" of Ings. The ideal number of things is " no-things," i.e.. *nothing*.

"Design" – The process of integrating a product's desired life cycle Ilities. Your must have the "owners" of these ilities as part of your team.

"Strategic Design" – A methodology, with related tools and measurements, for maximizing Ilities and minimizing Ings at the early product concept stage.

The Principles of Strategic Design

1. A product is the sum of its life cycle processes, or Ings, not its manufactured parts.

Every design sets in motion a torrent of tasks required for creating, manufacturing, servicing, and disposing of a product. Manufacturing the physical parts of a product is only a small fraction of these life cycle tasks, or Ings.

Understanding the total complexity of these tasks and simplifying those which can give your customer, and yourself, the greatest benefit can give you a winning advantage.

For example, Apple Computer's success can be traced to its early ability to reduce the number of learning Ings their users had to suffer. Apple simplified the learning tasks and quickly gained a wide following. They made personal computing "user friendly".

Design improvement tools in recent years have focused on the factory floor. Such tools as "design for assembly" or "design for manufacture" emphasize the importance of visible factory product cost. But this may not be where you can gain the greatest advantage.

What is not well understood are the hidden Ings, all of the life cycle "front-to-back" processes, activities and tasks required to create, support, and integrate these parts and products. Conventional accounting methods do a poor job of capturing the real cost of a product.

Only material and direct "touch" labor are gathered on a product-by-product basis. "Indirect expense" such as overhead and "burden" is gathered in the aggregate and "allocated" to labor for financial accounting purposes. These expenses can account for 40%, or even more, of a product's manufactured cost. These Ings are "hidden" from the view of the product design team and are not made part of the design equation.

For example, many companies sent component contracts overseas, based on lower labor rates. In many cases, the savings of lower labor rates was more than offset by the indirect "hidden" costs of time delays, shipping costs, paperwork and other "overheads."

Conventional accounting methods offer little help to a product design team in understanding how to reduce these hidden Ings, both on their own factory floor as well on the floors of its suppliers and customers.

The result: design team ignores these critical Ings even though they are the toughest cost problems today.

2. **All Ilities must be considered concurrently beginning on "Day One" of the design effort.**

All designs are "trade offs". There is no such thing as a "perfect" design. All product attributes, or Ilities must be balanced against one another, with the eventual product design being a compromise.

The best place to understand all these ilities and begin the trade-off process is at the early concept stage. This is when the design is flexible and changes can be made with an eraser or the stroke of a pen on a computer screen.

By identifying and making these trade-offs early, you can slash months from your product development schedule. You can also avoid costly engineering changes.

Unfortunately, too often this is not the case. We focus on the technical attributes first and only later consider other life cycle Ilities, such as manufacturability, maintainability, and others.

For example, one design team failed to include a member of its service department on its early design concept team. The team spent six months developing their design only to discover that they had failed to consider several key service procedures.

Remember: Spend time up front to make sure you have surfaced all your Ilities.

3. **Maximize your Ilities, minimize your Ings.**

Follow this simple rule and you will be miles ahead of your competition. Your selection of Ilities, or product attributes, is key to meeting both your customer's, and your own, needs.

Spend time reaching out to find Ilities your competition may not even be considering. Go well beyond "customer requirements" to find benefits to separate your product from the competitive pack.

For example, Chrysler Corporation was one of the first automotive companies to spend considerable design time on driver "creature comforts", such as coffee cup holders. Other companies shunned them as trivial. Luxury car divisions even declared they detracted from the decor of their interiors.

When consumer studies showed coffee cup holders played a significant role in car purchases, other manufacturers jumped on board. Today even luxury car manufacturers feature them.

Moral of the story: Including even simple Ilities in your product can bring a major success.

If Ilities are what you want in a product, then Ings are what you want to avoid.

An Ing is any task required to create, manufacture, support or dispose of a product during its life span. Within your company Ings are such tasks as "designing, prototyping, machining, painting, packaging," and thousands more. Many of these Ings are ignored in making critical design decisions, such as "purchasing, supervising, inspecting," and others.

But your design also sets in motion Ings outside the walls of your company. On the supplier side these are "manufacturing, inspecting, shipping" while on the customer side they are "installing, maintaining, servicing, and disposing."

All Ings cost money, time and carry with them the potential of failure.

For example, the new SDRC Master Series was designed to maximize the technical Ilities a team requires to analyze its design. But, at the same time, the Master Series requires far less "learning", a very time-consuming and expensive task in the engineering field.

4. ***All visible Ings create additional hidden Ings, with some creating far more than others.***

While all visible Ings should be avoided, some Ings are far worse than others. These are the Ings which carry with them a myriad of tasks or activities, most hidden from the normal view of the product design team.

For example, machining a part requires tooling, operating the machine, and removing the scrap. Most of the Ings required by this kind of machining are captured quite well by accounting systems and are highly "visible" to your design teams.

But many other Ings are not so obvious.

Consider the example of painting. The painting was traditionally considered as a low cost process. Ask an accountant what a refrigerator costs to paint and he will give you a dollar figure based on material and labor, usually a very small percentage of the total product cost. His accounting system "captures" these costs quite accurately.

What his accounting system does not capture, however, is the "hidden" cost of painting. These are the indirect expense Ings of *storing* the paint (safely), *prepping* the painted surface, *masking* to avoid overspray, *protecting* both the environment and the people applying the paint, and *packaging* the painted surface so it won't be scratched.

Then there is the cost of *re-touching* a damaged surface or *removing* the packaging and *disposing* of it at the customer's site. The list of hidden ings required by painting is endless. Their total cost is many multiples times the visible, direct cost of the paint and the labor and machines to apply it. No wonder it is on the "hit list" of most manufacturing managers.

5. *A design effort without an "in-process" measurement system to guide it will finish last.*

In-process measurement is tracking design effort while it's underway, so that you have time to take corrective action. It is not "post-process" measurement, which is done after the design is complete and it is too late to make corrections and the "horse is out of the barn."

"In-process" measurement is done while the design is underway. It helps to keep you on course, pointing out reefs and shoals which could wreck your design effort.

Post design process measurement is valuable for analyzing a product's performance when it reaches the field. This information can then be used to improve future product designs. For example, studying a product's MTBF (mean time between failure) performance can go a long way in guiding a team's future design.

But you must also use in-process design measurement to take action before the "horse is out of the barn."

6. *Measure those Ilities which are most strategic to your product success.*

Product design teams perform as they are measured. Use the right measurements and you will get the right results. Use the wrong ones and the results can be disastrous.

Always measure the "critical few" Ilities which will help your team defeat your competition. But the sad fact is that most teams are measured in the wrong way, at the wrong time and for the wrong things.

Design teams usually are measured by their ability to achieve design goals in three categories:

    Schedule.   Is the design project on time?
    Performance. Are the technical specs being met?
    Direct Cost.   Is direct labor and material within budget?

These three "traditional" metrics are easily measured and can be tracked quite accurately.

But these three measurements reveal only a small part of a product's potential for success. Other Ilities may even be far more important than these three.

Take for example Company Y, a manufacturer of pumps. Its design team took great pride in meeting the three milestones noted above for a new centrifugal pump model. Schedule, performance and direct cost were all on target, in some cases even ahead of the target goals.

But the new Y product failed miserably within one year of introduction. What was the problem? The team failed to correctly design for fast serviceability, the amount of time required to replace a worn pump impeller.

Their competitor's new model could be serviced in 50% less time, a critical issue in keeping a pumping system "on line."

Serviceability time was not even measured as the new design progressed. The team had failed to track its most critical Ility.

7. *Measure for direction, not precision.*

A wise man once said, "Don't use a micrometer when a tape measure will do."

First focus on measuring whether your design is headed in the right direction at the early stages of your effort. Don't worry about the decimals.

Use Delphi, or consensus measurement, to keep you on track for some Ilities which are difficult to measure. The collective judgement of your team is far better than no measurement at all.

With the exception of your product's technical performance, very little about your design in its early stages can be measured with any degree of accuracy. But this does not mean you cannot measure.

8. *Good design is as much a social science as a technical science.*

Here is a good design rule: Focus first on designing your team dynamics, and then go to work on your product design.

Far more teams end up on the rocks from poor human dynamics than from a lack of technical expertise.

Avoid putting people on a team who are not socially skilled. They may be the best technical experts around, but if they have difficulty working within a group, they can poison your entire design effort.

After you have set your team "ground rules", use in-process measurement to track how efficiently your team is working. Monitoring how well your team "human dynamics" is on-track can surface problems while they are still manageable.

9. *Place Ility creation and Ing control in the hands of those who understand them best.*

Problems are best understood by those who suffer from them most. These people also have the greatest interest in solving them. And they usually have some excellent ideas for eliminating them.

That is why a multi-functional design team, properly trained and motivated, is so powerful.

Experience shows that management's most effective role is to set the broad boundaries of a new product effort.

The responsibility for creating all the intermediate "ility" goals should be the task of the design team. This builds goal "ownership".

Your design team should also have the task of creating the measurement system for tracking these goals. Goals without measurements are rarely reached.

Of course, both the team goals as well as the measurements must be also "owned" by management.

The Strategic Design Method, described in the next chapter, gives you a step-by-step way of building goals and measurements "from the ground up."

10. Be cautious with design "tools", they can "kill" you.

Using a wrench to drive a nail can cause you a lot of pain. The same is true of design tools. Too many design teams rush to use the wrong tools, at the wrong time and in the wrong way.

For example, many companies in the past rushed to use computer-based tools without really giving enough thought to their fundamental purpose. Designs were detailed more quickly, but were fundamentally still flawed.

In other cases, design teams have rated the quality of their new design based on design-for-assembly or manufacturability tools, only to realize too late that these were not really the competitive issues.

For example, one Motorola division used a computer-based design-for-assembly tool that rated the quality of a design on its part count and assembly time.

A deadly race began to eliminate as many parts as possible, with the focus being on easy targets such as screws, nuts, washers and bolts to gain better "DFA rating." Snap fit fastening became the rule of the day.

Only later did this division realize that snap fits were causing tooling costs to skyrocket and development times to lengthen. While direct labor was reduced, their "hidden" indirect costs began to explode.

The first tools to use in your design effort must be the "thinking" ones, used at the early product concept stage. These tools help your design team head in the right direction. They help you find the right problems to solve.

Concept stage tools should be easy to learn by the entire team, have a metric attached to know if they are working, and usable only with the entire team in place so that they build common understanding and buy-in.

The opposite of this kind of tool is one which is useable only by an "expert" as well as difficult to learn. These tools do little to help solve the social dynamics problems of having your design team working in unity from the start.

11. Seek the root causes of life cycle problems and cure them by design so they don't reappear again.

All problems have root causes. Too often we waste time and resources attacking problems at the "effect" stage, where we finally experience them, rather than at their "cause" stage.

The task of your design team must be to analyze these "effects" and trace them to their design roots. The reason for a multi-functional design team is to better understand all these product life cycle problems and their causes. The process owners of these painful Ings are best qualified for this task.

Unfortunately, the Western industrial world has wasted much time and money attempting to solve problems too late and in the wrong place, only to awaken later to the real causes of these problems.

For example, the quality improvement effort in America began on the factory floor. Quality leaders such as Deming and others introduced tools to identify and track poor quality processes. Such techniques as statistical process control (SPC) track the performance of a manufacturing process to understand when it is "out of control" and how to correct it.

Today we still use these factory floor quality tools but we are beginning to understand that the best cure for a poor manufacturing process is its simplification, or even elimination, at the design phase.

The ideal solution is to design the problem out before it even appears on the manufacturing floor.

12. The goal of design first must be to seek problems, not solutions.

Solving problems is only part of the design task. Too many hard-working design teams fail because they worked on the wrong problem at the wrong time and in the wrong way.

The first task is to seek problems to solve beyond those requested by your customer and currently being addressed by your competitor. Identifying and solving such opportunities can give you competitive advantage.

Most new concurrent design teams have very poor design skills. This is understandable since most on such a team have never before directly participated in the design process.

But, unfortunately, many product designers have underdeveloped design skills. They may have excellent engineering skills, but engineering is not design.

The engineering process takes a set of technical requirements and works them to a solution. The design process seeks new problems to solve, many of which are not even technical. The design process creates a product success equation far beyond the technical issues.

Too many design teams unknowingly shrink their design boundaries in the early, creative concept stage. They focus on those problems which are well understood. They miss the opportunity to go "out of bounds" to find new ways to please customers, improve profits and be a major winner.

Like all human beings, we spend most of our time working on problems we understand well and can measure well. This is despite the fact that problems which are now understood well and cannot be measured accurately are the ones which kill us in business as well as our private lives.

Chapter Summary

In this chapter, you learned the twelve key principles that are at the core of the Strategic Design method. These principles focus on the need to use new methodology, new measurements and new management techniques if we are really to improve the product design process.

In the next chapter, you will learn how to develop a Strategic Design brief, a powerful tool for applying these principles at the very start of your design effort.

Chapter 5.

How To Start Your Concurrent Design Effort

Old methods yield old results.

Nowhere is this more true than in the world of product design. The great failures of most concurrent engineering teams can be traced to their lack of a design method to guide them to a competitive solution.

The **Strategic Design Method,** described in this chapter, gives you a step-by-step way to harness the full horsepower of your multi-functional design team. It guarantees that you will cover "all the bases" in finding your optimum design solution. It makes sure that all the "voices" of the entire team are being heard. And it builds senior management confidence in your final decision.

Your design team needs only 24 working hours, or about three days, to apply this powerful method by preparing a **Strategic Design Brief.** This is best done at the start of your design effort, but can later be applied at any stage in your product development.

Here is what developing a **Strategic Design Brief** will do for you:
1. Define the design problem with agreement of all, including management.
2. Shape a strategy framework to guide your design thinking.
3. Generate creative design solutions.
4. Develop a design measurement system
5. Create a "next steps" action plan.

At the end of the 24 hours you will have a written document clearly showing how you made your decisions, ready for review by management for their buy-in. The methodology gives you a "road map" for writing this document.

The Stategic Design Method was developed and refined exclusively for Concurrent Engineering teams over the past 11 years. It integrates both technical content and team process.

Strategic Design helps you find the correct design decision and, at the same time, builds support for its implementation. As every successful facilitator knows, one without the other is useless. The Strategic Design Brief captures these thoughts, in writing, for your design team, management as well as other teams.

Strategic Design is used at the early concept stage of your design process. It is this phase which "drives" 70%, or more, of cost, quality, and time-to-market. The concept stage includes everything your team does up to the point when it begins detailing the individual parts in your product.

No Conflict With Your Present Tools

Strategic Design is not a substitute for the stage-by-stage product delivery system you already have in place. It is used in front of your present product delivery process.

It guides your team in developing a "quick start" for your design effort.

Very importantly, Strategic Design gives your team, and management, a rating system for measuring how well your design is meeting objectives.

Stategic Design is not a replacement for design tools such as Quality Function Deployment (QFD), Design of Experiments (DOE), Design for Manufacturability (DFM) or others. It is used in advance of these tools. In fact, it helps your design team decide which of these tools should be used, why and when. It helps you avoid using one of these tools in the wrong way and at the wrong time.

Your Strategic Design Road Map

Your guide to building your Strategic Design Brief is the method's Road Map, a five-step process used to guide your team through its intensive 24-working hour task. The two key road map elements are *iteration and integration*.

The Road Map is iterative. It requires that your team rotate through it several times. This *process of iteration* is a classical feature of all good problem definition and solving methodologies. Each clockwise iteration through the Road Map will help you reveal problems not seen before.

These will, in turn, trigger new solutions to make your design effort even more effective. The bottom line: Your team will gain more confidence in their final solution.

The Road Map is also **integrative**. It enables you to build strong management support for your design effort, right from the start of your effort. The Road Map helps you gain management buy-in every step of the way by making them part of the concept stage decision-making process. It also builds stronger commitment on the part of each member of your team, as well as stronger backup by their "home" functional departments.

The following overview will give you a quick introduction in how the Strategic Design works. Each step outlined below is supported by a set of tools unique to the methodology. Later chapters will go into more depth on some of these major tools.

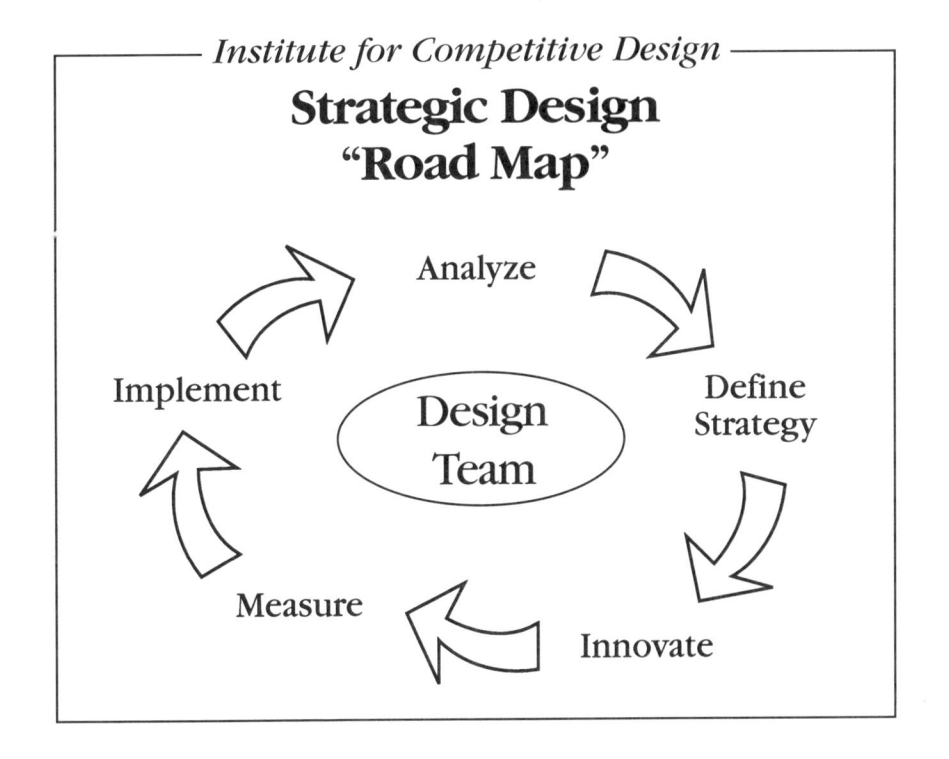

Institute for Competitive Design

Strategic Design "Road Map"

Analyze → Define Strategy → Innovate → Measure → Implement → (Analyze)

Design Team

41

Additional tools can be found in the ICD publication "Strategic Design: A Concurrent Engineering Handbook."

How To Prepare A Strategic Design Brief

The **Strategic Design Brief** is your design team's "deliverable" at the end of their 24 hour effort. It is a document developed, and "owned", by the entire team. The maximum recommended length is no more than 25 total pages.

Here are the five sections it contains:

> **Section 1.** A brief statement of the product opportunity in terms of functions required, design boundaries, internal capabilities, and the competitive environment.
>
> Content: 4-6 pages
>
> **Section 2.** A clear statement of the team's design strategy, including the eight (8) key Ilities they will focus on, including quantitative goals for each, and a rating system to measure the design effort.
>
> Content: 4-6 pages
>
> **Section 3.** "First effort" design alternatives, including sketches and supporting information
>
> Content: 3-6 pages
>
> **Section 4.** A comparative measurement of each design alternative, including how well each meets the team's 8-point Ility strategy.
>
> Content: 2-3 pages
>
> **Section 5.** An implementation action plan the team has agreed to for "next steps."
>
> Content: 3-4 pages

Completion of the Design Brief indicates concurrence by your entire design team on these major issues. All unresolved issues are included as part of the Action Plan section for later work.

Immediately following the 24-hour session, your design team presents their Design Brief to management. The purpose is to gain their buy-in on the thinking of the team.

Presentation to Management

The goal of your management presentation is to build "upward" integration. Too often management plays little or no direct role in shaping the early conceptual design stage, opting to wait until prototype stage when there is "something to see".

Anxious to "get on" with the product development many managers, and teams, rush to leave the conceptual stage too early. The result is a flawed conceptual design with the flaws only becoming known at the later prototype stage. The price is expensive engineering changes, slipped schedules, frayed nerves and shattered budgets.

Presentation of your team's Strategic Design Brief to management builds buy-in from the start. The Brief brings content, structure, measurement and dialogue to the formative conceptual design stage. It integrates management into the design process, drawing on their expertise and vision.

Differences between your design team and management can be "ironed out" with a minimum of chaos and cost.

This management presentation should be made by the entire team immediately following the 24 hours of preparing the Design Brief. How much later? My experience shows it should be made within weeks.

Here are six reasons why you will immediately benefit from preparing a Strategic Design Brief:

> **1. Intensity.** The 24-hour time limit focuses team effort on the critical design issues. They have little time to waste on non-critical issues.
>
> **2. Efficiency.** Your team quickly finds they must design an efficient team dynamics process if they are to meet their deadline. They clearly understand the rule "Design your team process before your begin to design your product."

3. Cooperation. They soon learn they must break down their team into cooperative sub-teams if they are ever to make the deadline.

4. Communication. Your team builds stronger interpersonal communication links which will pay-off later as they begin to implement their design.

5. Integration. All team members simultaneously gain a better perspective of the big picture. All members have an opportunity to be heard.

6. Ownership. The entire team must "sign on" to the design concept before it is presented to management. This helps build commitment.

7. Direction. The Strategic Design Brief gives clear "next steps" direction for both the team and management. Should there be major problems of disagreement, either within the team or with management, these points are clearly known and must be addressed before the design effort can move forward.

Steps In Preparing A Strategic Design Brief

Step I. Discover Your Business Opportunity

Competitive design is more than just solving your customer's known problems. It is going beyond these to find new problems he may not even anticipate. It is also about solving many of your own, internal company problems at the same time. Your team's first design task is to make sure you are solving the right set of problems, in the right way, and at the right time. You must discover the dimensions of your total business opportunity.

Task 1. Define "core" product functions

Ask your design team to brainstorm your basic product functions on three levels: *System* — What is the "core" or basic function of your customer's system or product?

Product — What is the "core" function of the product you will deliver? *Parts* — What are the functions of each part in your present (or first iteration) design?

Limit these "What" descriptions of "System" and "Product" to 25 words, or less. Focus on the single, essential function wanted by the customer. Elegant designs are simple designs. This exercise gets your team back to basics. Use a "verb-noun" format to write down individual part functions. Remember all parts have more than one function. This exercise makes sure you do not include useless functions, or forget some, in your design. It also gives your entire team a better understanding of your product. Make sure you reach team consensus on all these functions.

Task 2. Set Your Product Design Boundaries

Clarify your design boundaries. Get down in writing where you think you can go — and can't go. First look at *external boundaries* such as customer requirements, government regulations, supply constraints, and marketplace conditions. Then review *internal boundaries* such as company policies, financial constraints and strategic goals. Especially review the *product development goals* outlined by your senior management to your team. Does your team really "buy into" them? Challenge all boundaries to better understand them and perhaps even change them. Don't accept any as "given." Too many teams define their design boundaries too tightly, preventing them from finding new, innovative solutions. At other times, management's goals may be far lower than those your team thinks it can really accomplish.

Task 3. Assess Your Company Capabilities

This is when your team determines your company's real capabilities, both positive and negative. Learn what you are really competitive at doing. Ask each team member to report out on his department's strength's and weaknesses.

Compile these as a written "capabilities assessment." Smart design is the ability to develop a product which favors your company's strengths and limits exposing your weaknesses.

Task 4. Identify your competitive environment. Know your direct competitors and their product lines. Analyze their strengths and weaknesses. One of your goals will be to design to attack their weak points. But then go well beyond your competition to understand market forces that could influence the future success of your design. And learn about any competitive technologies that could be a threat in the future. Get this competitive assessment down on paper for team buy-in.

Task 5. Gain management approval of your definition of the business problem as developed in Steps 1-4. Begin writing your team Strategic Design Brief outlining your combined thinking on the four key issues discussed above. These basic assumptions will shape your team's decision-making. You must be sure they are in line with management's thinking. This helps you avoid confusion and problems later. It will also build management confidence in your team.

Step II. Define Your Design Strategy

There will be many ways for your team to design a product. Each will have its individual merits. Your goal is to find the *optimum* solution, for both the customer and your company. Your solution must be able to simultaneously meet your customer's requirements as well as your company's needs.

Defining a design strategy focuses the efforts of your team on the "strategic few", those attributes, or Ilities, that will make your team a competitive winner. Too many design teams do not think strategically about the total business problem. Instead, they think in terms of technical problem solving. Multi-functional team design gives you a unique insight to "see the big picture" from the total business perspective.

The steps overviewed below will guide you in defining your optimum strategy. See Chapter 7, "Maximizing Your Ilities: How to Build A Design Strategy" for a detailed explanation of each step, as well as examples for each.

Task 1. Brainstorm and agree on the eight (8) key Ilities which will give you a competitive edge over your competition. Try to limit your list to eight as this is about the maximum a team can focus on effectively at one given time. Think *strategically*. What Ility will give you the greatest advantage? Go well beyond your customer's stated requirements or Ilities to find those your competition may not even be considering in their design equation.

Task 2. Develop a "core" definition for each of your eight strategic Ilities. Limit your scope. Try to use 25 words, or less, to simplify your definition. Make sure everyone on your team understands and "buys into" each of them.

Task 3. Assign quantifiable goals for each Ility. Remember the old adage: "If you can't count it, it doesn't count." Quantifiable goals, or "metrics", are important in telling you how far you have to go and whether you are heading in the right direction. Strive for direction, not precision in setting these goals. Remember that you are in the early stages of your concept development. They can always be modified during later design iterations.

Task 4. Rank and weigh each of your strategic Ilities. Rank highest those which will directly benefit your customer. Develop a weighting system to show the relative importance of each Ility for your product's success. Document your team's reasoning for each in your Strategic Design Brief.

Task 5. Begin brainstorming a list of design Ility drivers for each of your strategic Ilities. Look for "root cause" indicators which show you are headed in the right direction. For example, designing for "serviceability" can mean the specification of standard, off-the-shelf parts, no tools required, high wear parts designed in where they are most accessible, few or no service instructions required and other Ility drivers.

Task 6. Build a "Spider" measurement chart to baseline each of your strategic Ilities and simultaneously track them throughout your conceptual design process. (See Chapter 7 for an explanation of the ICD "Spider Chart" tool). Baseline where your present "starting point" is now, i.e. based on an existing design, your competitor's design or your latest design iteration. Quantify each baseline point as best you can. Include your strategy measurement chart in your Strategic Design Brief.

Task 7. Share your strategy with management and discuss any differences of opinion. Make sure you review your Spider Chart then as it will serve as a major measurement of your design success. Gain management's approval of your total design strategy before beginning your design innovation process.

Step III. Innovate Strategic Solutions

Innovation is the "fun" phase of product design. But innovation without strategic direction is a waste of time. Keep your team on-track by focusing them on the key strategic Ilities they identified earlier and have documented in their Strategic Design Brief. Encourage them to see their product as more than just an assembly of parts. Help them see their product as a *system* of all the steps (Ings) required to design, manufacture, purchase and field support it. This systems thinking is the key to elegant, competitive design today. Maximize your Ilities and minimize your Ings.

Task 1. Have your team "map" all the major tasks, or Ings required by your present product design or the first iteration of your new design. Get your team thinking *globally*. Are they clearly aware of all the supplier side tasks? What about customer Ings, or tasks?

Task 2. Begin to iterate your design many times. Review your Ility drivers list and generate starting solutions. Encourage open discussion and "no negatives" brainstorming.

Task 3. Periodically ask your team to chart their Ility results. Remind them that all designs are trade-offs and that there is no such thing as a "perfect" solution. Using the "Spider Chart" to track design iterations keeps the team focused on their strategic goals.

Task 4. Continue to develop global Ing maps to reveal design, or process task complexity. Constantly encourage your team to look beyond product function and parts to see the total "cradle to grave" *system* the design concept would set in motion. Especially have your team measure their design's potential for creating "hidden" indirect cost or "overhead".

Step IV. Measure Your Results

Too many design efforts fail because of flawed measurements. The traditional "big three" measurements of "functional performance, project timetable, and direct cost" are easily tracked but do not reveal whether the product will be truly competitive. As managers, we generally focus on what we can measure best, even though these factors may not decide our success. A fundamental rule of good concurrent engineering is to have your design team develop their own *in-process* measurements and a tool to track them, such as the "Spider Chart" described in Chapter 7. At this stage of the Strategic Design Road Map your team should begin to apply these in-process measurements to improve their design.

Task 1. Plot your latest design on your Strategic Design Spider Chart. Clearly show your baseline "starting points" for each Ility. Develop sub-charts to show where you are for major Ilities. For example, you can develop a sub-chart for "manufacturability" with each of the eight legs representing one manufacturing "driver" such as part count, process steps, tooling cost, direct part cost, etc. Make sure you have complete team consensus on all of these. Be prepared to support your position on each "leg".

Task 2. Document the quality of your *team dynamics* to date. This tool is described in Chapter 9. Where are you in terms of schedule? What evidence do you have that your "team process" is on-track? Are consensus decisions being made quickly? Are there any human stumbling blocks hindering your progress? Summarize these in writing in your Strategic Design Brief.

Task 3. Identify re-design opportunities. Review your basic design opportunity assumptions. Were they correct? Re-focus your team on their key strategic Ilities. Were they the right ones? Change them if necessary. Your design iteration process will shed new light on all your previous assumptions. Be flexible enough to change your strategy if the team feels it worthwhile.

Task 4. Share your progress with management. Show them your in-process metrics for design performance, as well as your overall team dynamics performance. Communicate not only where you are with the "big three", technical performance, timetable, and direct cost, but show them your strategic design results using your Spider Chart. Show them how your design reduces the potential for high indirect, or "hidden" cost. Document your results in your team Strategic Design Brief.

Step V. Develop Your Team Action Plan

The Ilities and Ings your team imbeds in their design will directly influence the timing, cost and quality of your total design effort. The more complex the design, the more time your team must spend developing it. For example, the specification of an immature manufacturing process in your design will mean more validation time will be required during the design prove-out stage.

Designs with many variable processes require more documentation to make sure tests are in place to control the variation. And designs requiring close precision tolerances may require new tooling. The purpose of this stage in the Strategic Design Process Road Map is to review your total product development plan against your latest design iteration. Does your design fit the time line of your initial action plan? Which should change? The design? The implementation time line? Perhaps both?

Task 1. Map your total design implementation plan using the time requirements required by your latest design iteration. Compare this to your original implementation plan. Look for problem areas. Your constant goal should be to shrink design time.

Task 2. Identify any major "time drivers" created by your latest design. Candidly discuss with your team how to reduce the impact of these time drivers. In the case of special tooling, for example, would it be possible to order tool steel ahead of finishing the final part design? Could an important test procedure be completed by outside resources to avoid waiting for scarce in-company resources already committed to another project?

Task 3. Simplify your design process. Look at opportunities to reduce the overall complexity of your latest design and thus compress implementation time and cost. Focus on simplifying your design Ings. Make sure both your "core" and "second ring", or part-time, design team participates in this process. Second ring team members usually can identify valid "shortcuts" for compressing design time.

Task 4. Gain management's approval of your revised action plan. Your goal should be to *compress*, not extend your schedule. Be ready to support any changes. Remember to update your Strategic Design Brief. Be prepared to iterate your design again through the Strategic Process Design Road Map.

Chapter Summary

In this chapter, you learned how to start your concurrent design effort by preparing a Strategic Design Brief, a powerful tool for building understanding and agreement at the very beginning of your design effort.

The Strategic Design Brief integrates your design team's thinking about what basic design strategy they will follow and how they will measure success. It also integrates management into the process by giving them a step-by-step role for "buying into" the team's design decisions.

In the next chapter, you will learn why you must create your own, customized measurement tools for tracking your team's design "in-process", while it is underway. Unlike "post-process" tools, these help your team correct mistakes early in their product development process.

Chapter 6.

Why You Must Use In-Process Measurements And Tools To Keep On Track

This chapter gives you the "ground rules" for both design measurements and tools. Too many design teams use the wrong measurements and the wrong tools and get poor results.

Effective design tools head you in the direction of the right design solution. Effective design measurements tell you how well you are doing. Linked together, they are a powerful combination.

The following chapters will give you step-by-step instruction in how to use these measurements and tools to make your design effort a true winner.

First, I will cover the rules for design measurement. Then I will move on to describe what tools work best and why.

Measure "In-Process"

Product teams perform as they measure, as well as how they are measured by others. We usually measure the wrong things, at the wrong time, and hence get the wrong results.

The most powerful kind of measurements are those we use **"in-process."** These are the measurements which help guide us to success while there is still plenty of time for design corrections.

The opposite of an "in-process" measurement is a **"post-process"** one. Post-process measurements tell us what went wrong so that, hopefully, we won't make the same mistake "next time."

The first measurement task of your design team must be to identify what Ilities are absolutely essential for your product's success. The second task is to set up an in-process measurement system for these key Ilities.

Is it "installability?" A cellular telephone manufacturer develops a product which you can install in your car within five minutes with absolutely no drilling required. This is in contrast to having a professional installer doing the job for $150. The cellular telephone manufacturer's market share skyrockets.

Or is it "deliverability?" A pizza maker builds his product around time and convenience, promising delivery to your home within 20 minutes. While other pizza companies struggle with new recipes to build market share, the fast delivery company becomes a billion dollar corporation.

Go Beyond the "Common Three"

We don't take enough time to develop a set of "metrics," or measurements, to track what is strategically important. Instead we continue to focus on the "common three":

1. Schedule: Is the project on time?
2. Performance: Are all technical requirements being met?
3. Direct Cost: Is the product's material and labor expense in line with projections?

While schedule, technical performance and budget are all important for your product's success, just reaching them does not guarantee that your product will be a commercial success.

Schedule pressure, especially artificially-fixed milestones not set by the design team, can sometimes do more harm than good.

For example, one design team was under such schedule pressure that they decided to avoid every new approach which might require additional time for design validation and testing. The product made it to market on time but was a watered-down product which soon failed in their highly competitive marketplace.

Technical performance criteria also must be met but that does not guarantee success in the marketplace. The brief history of Silicon Valley is full of examples of companies which met technical performance requirements but were not able to move this into the marketplace quickly and at low cost.

Direct cost, the cost of labor and material, is the poorest measurement of the three. Labor and material cost today is shrinking as a percentage of product's total life cycle cost. We are now recognizing the importance of slashing indirect costs such as overhead, and post-factory costs, such as product installation, customer maintenance, and disposal.

Strive For Design Direction

Why do we focus only on these traditional three measurements? The answer is that they are both well-understood and easily measureable.

We focus on those problems we understand and can measure well. This is despite the fact that the problems we don't understand well, and find difficult to measure, are the ones that can kill us in a product.

We also seem to feel that precision is an indicator of validity and value in measurement. Many technically-minded design team members have a fixation on the accuracy of measurement, as though anything which cannot be measured to a four-place decimal should not be considered a valid measurement.

Too often we demand the same precision we find in the technical world for the business world. And when this is impossible, we simply don't measure.

What's worse, we may forgo measuring while the design is being developed, feeling it is impossible to do and deciding to wait until the design is complete, when it is really too late to do anything with the measurement information. In short, when "the horse is out of the barn."

The Strategic Design Method is based on using in-process measurement of all your design's strategic Ilities, the ones which will make you and your design team a winner.

The Two "Musts"

Your must measure in-process two key elements:

1. **Your Product.** Is it on track in terms of quality, total time, and life cycle cost? Is it meeting your customer's key Ility needs? Equally important, is your product meeting your company's Ility needs, such as profitability?
2. **Your Team Design Process.** Is your team working efficiently? Are you harnessing the full power of concurrent design?

Here are the basic measurement rules you must know and apply.

Strategic Design Measurement Rules

1. Measure in-process while you are developing the design. Begin at the early concept stage.
2. Measure what is important, focusing on your key competitive Ilities.
3. Strive for design direction, not precision of measurement. Measurement accuracy does not assure that you are headed in the right direction.
4. Measure often. This helps focus your effort and keeps your team on track.
5. Allow the design team to develop and propose their own measurements. They will both believe in them and use them.
6. Measure both product and team process. Success in the first is difficult without success in the second.

What Design Tools Work Best?

Reaching your Ility goals requires using the right design tools.

Today we are constantly exposed to a widening variety of design tools. Design of Experiments (DOE). Taguchi Methods. Design for Manufacturability and Assembleability (DFMA). Quality Function Deployment (QFD). The "alphabet soup" of design tools seems to be getting thicker every day.

Many are of Japanese origin. Originally used in Japan by successful manufacturers, they are now being imported by the West with great hope and expectation.

I have never encountered a design tool I have not respected. All have great potential. This chapter will tell you which tools work best and why. It sets forth a clear set of rules for design tools.

Why Some Tools Fail

Unfortunately, too many design tools get a black eye because they are used at the wrong time and in the wrong way. Teams use Design for Manufacturability (DFM) tools to slash manufacturing cost, only to discover later they could have been farther ahead by improving the product's field serviceability.

Others have used Quality Function Deployment (QFD) in listening to the "voice of the customer" only to awaken months later to the fact they were listening to the wrong customer.

All of these tools are powerful when used at the right time and in the right way. But it's the mis-application of these tools which can get us in serious trouble.

Tools Must Build Team Buy-In

The most powerful design tools are the ones which help both improve the product and the team's social dynamics.

For example, during the early stages of design use easy-to-learn tools which bring all your product's major Ilities quickly into focus. Avoid using specialized, hard-to-learn tools which require a lot of time and are difficult to apply.

Types of Design Tools

There are fundamentally three types of design tools:

Efficiency Tools. These tools help us implement a conceptual design faster, at lower cost, and with fewer communication mistakes. Examples of these are computer-aided design tools which help us visualize a design better, as well as automate its implementation. Others include rapid prototyping tools to quickly produce a product model. These efficiency tools are post-concept stage ones, used when we are quite confident in our design approach. Industry has invested millions in such tools.

Problem-Solving Tools. These tools help us solve well-defined technical problems. Examples include mold flow analysis for injection molding problems, stress analysis tools, and simulation tools such as solids modeling. Others include Design for Manufacturability (DFM) with its focus on solving the challenge of making a product and its related parts more produceable. These problem-solving tools help assure we will reach the right conclusion to known problems.

Conceptual Design Tools. These tools are used at the early design stage to first seek the right problems to solve in the right way and at the right time. There are very few of these tools available to a design team today.

Strategic Design and its related tool set are these kinds of tools. They help your design team do their job right from the start.

Unfortunately, industry has invested heavily in both design efficiency and design problem-solving tools with sometimes questionable paybacks. Very little expense is being invested in the early concept stage, where more than 70% of a design's cost, quality, and time-to-market is set in motion. Strategic Design and its accompanying tool set was developed to help you correct this flaw.

Strategic Design tools are conceptual tools. The Stategic Design Method is used in the early design concept stage, ahead of such tools as Quality Function Deployment, Design of Experiments, Design For Manufacturability, and others. While these are valuable problem-solving tools for refining a product design, they do not concurrently help you develop your total design concept, both from the technical and commercial aspects.

These tools help solve specific design problems. But they do little to help the team look for new problems to solve in different ways. They focus rather than expand. The concept stage of design requires problem-seeking first, and problem-solving second.

Rules For Design Concept Tools

1. Keep them simple. Tools which are easily learned are easily remembered...and used.
2. Use tools which concurrently address all the Ilities. Don't use a tool which focuses too early on one Ility. You may be headed in the wrong direction.
3. Use only those which are totally team-oriented. Avoid tools which only an "expert" understands and can use. Your team will usually distrust both the tool and the expert.
4. Provide a measurement, or "metric" with each tool. You need this to tell you if the tool is "working".
5. Use tools which fit your organizational culture. What works for one company may not work for another.
6. Use tools which are fast. Avoid detailed, time-consuming ones. Strive for direction, not detail, in the early design concept stage.

All Strategic Design tools meet the above criteria.

Chapter Summary

In this chapter, you learned the ground rules for design measurement and tools. Using the right design tools heads you in the direction of the best product solution. Using timely design measurement tells you how well you are doing. Linked together, measurements and tools are a powerful combination.

In the next chapter, you will learn a tool for identifying what Ilities your design must deliver to be a winner, as well as how to set quantifiable goals for each. You will also learn how to build a measurement tool to make sure your team is on-track in meeting these goals.

Chapter 7.

Maximizing Your Ilities: How To Build a Design Strategy

Winning design teams think strategically. They focus on Ilities which will put their product well ahead of the competitive pack.

They are constantly thinking in a total business dimension, not just about technical requirements. Their design equation encompasses benefits their customers may not even expect and that their competitors may not even be thinking about. Winning teams think strategically.

Unfortunately, too many design teams rush to solve technical product performance problems, missing opportunities in other Ility areas. Other teams skip the strategy shaping process entirely. Still others develop a design strategy, but fail to share it with management, only to discover its flaws late in the product development process.

In chapter 5 you were given an overview of how to start your design effort by quickly preparing a Design Brief, using the Strategic Design Method.

This chapter gives you step-by-step direction in one of your most critical tasks, developing your design strategy and shaping a measurement system for it.

You will learn how to:

1. Develop an eight-point product Ility strategy with measurable goals.
2. Identify the design drivers to help you accomplish these goals.
3. Build an easy-to-use measurement tool to keep your design team on-track, as well as communicate effectively with management.

What Is a Design Strategy?

A design strategy is the team's definition of what the product must do to delight the customer, defeat the competition, and, at the same time, meet internal company goals.

It is a clearly-stated set of product goals and measurements to guide the team through the design delivery process. Both the goals and the measurements are agreed upon by the entire team, as well as endorsed by management. Most of the specific strategy goals are set by the entire multi-functional design team.

Defining a design strategy is done during the 24-hour working time period set by the Strategic Design Method. Roughed out during the first eight hours, it is later refined throughout the remaining hours as the design is better understood.

Here is a task-by-task overview of how to develop a Strategic Design strategy.

How To Build a Design Strategy

To do these tasks well, you must have your entire multi-functional team in place. Strategic advantage can come from recognizing new opportunities throughout the product future life span, both internally and externally.

Team Task 1. Ility Selection

Systematically discuss each of the four Global Opportunity Quadrants (see Chapter 3 for a review of this concept). Always begin this brainstorming process by **focusing on customer Ilities first.**

Remember: You will be unable to do this without having your marketing, sales, and field service process owners in this crucial meeting.

Always feel free to invent new Ility words to describe your strategic goals. Then get all your fellow team members to help define these Ilities. This is far better than using old terms with each team member having a different definition in mind.

Review the Ility list at the end of this chapter to jump start your thinking.

For example:

Customer Quadrant: Can we gain competitive advantage by focusing on installability, the time required to integrate our product into our customer's product? Are there opportunities to improve serviceability?

Design Quadrant: Are there any opportunities in the performance area? What about energy requirements? Should power consumeability be at the top of the list? Should the basic design be changed?

Factory Quadrant: Is manufacturability an issue? Should we focus on easy assembleability? What about the idea of imprecisionability, the goal of removing as much precision from the manufacturing process as possible.

Supply Quadrant: Should we look for competitive advantage by better supplier integration? What about component deliverability, the goal of just-in-time parts delivery?

Brainstorm many, but finally decide on eight Ilities. Why eight? My experience has shown this number is at the limit of what a multi-functional team can trade-off at one time. Focusing on eight enables your team to concentrate on the important few, not the trivial many.

Team Task 2. Definition and Goal Setting

Define each of your eight Ilities and then set quantifiable goals for each. Try to use 25 words, or less. Be as descriptive as possible. Avoid "umbrella" words such as produceability or manufacturability. These say little, and can have multiple meanings leading to confusion among your team members.

Here are four Ility examples, using the design of a refrigerator compressor as an example.

Installability. (External Customer Quadrant)

"Compressor mounting done with no brazing, all Z-axis motions, and 50% reduction in skill level required."

Goal: 75% reduction in installation time.

Designability. (Internal Design Quadrant)

"Use of current reciprocating compressor design with no new materials but different manufacturing processes and sequences, yet 20% improvement in energy consumption."

Goal: Design complete and validated in 6 months.

Assembleability. (Internal Factory Quadrant)

"All Z-axis assembly motions, no adjustments and a 50% reduction in total assembly time, including wait time."

Goal: 50% reduction in total assembly cycle time.

Deliverability. (External Supplier Quadrant)

"Just-in-time delivery of compressor housing castings with no more than a four-hour stock for all models on hand at one time."

Goal: One common housing casting for all models.

Team Task 3. Ranking Ilities

Put your eight Ilities in a rank order of importance. This builds team agreement on priorities when looking at alternate design solutions. You may even wish to apply a weighting factor to each of the eight.

In our compressor example, the team put designability at the top. Customers were demanding lower energy consumption immediately due to new governmental regulations.

Team Task 4. Building Cause & Effect Drivers

Brainstorm design cause-product effect drivers for each of the eight key Ilities. The best technique is to have your team members break into smaller groups for this task. Following are examples.

Installability (Supplier Quadrant)

Design Drivers:

- Fewer parts in design
- Less assembly steps
- No special tools
- Minimum training for assemblers
- Use of non-variable assembly processes
- Murphy proof

Deliverability (Supplier Quadrant)

- No change in casting material
- No change in supplier casting process
- One standard, re-usable shipping container
- Relaxation of tight tolerances
- Casting design complete within 90 days
- Supplier as member of design team

This cause and effect brainstorming process sets the stage for product innovation without "closing the blinders." Team members are encouraged to build as wide a list as possible, to expand their thinking.

Team Task 5. Building Your Measurement Tool

You are now ready to build a Strategic Design Ility "spider" chart. This is the final step in developing your strategy, and is one of the most important.

Your Ility chart captures all the key strategy positions taken by your design team. The chart serves to help build consensus, not only within your team but with management as well. The Ility chart later must be approved by management.

The Ility chart will also later be used by your team to rate designs as they begin their full-scale design effort.

An Ility chart meets all the measurement rules outlined in Chapter 6. It is easily understood, can be used to measure your design in-process, and is built by those who will be using it. It is an integration tool which requires the full participation of all the product's future process owners, as well as management.

The Ility chart's three purposes are:
1. Build agreement on key strategic design goals
2. Gain consensus of management
3. Rate alternate design solutions

The Five Steps In Building a Strategic Design Ility Chart

Following is a quick overview of how to build a Strategic Design Ility Chart.

Step One: Identify your key 8 Ilities in rank order

Using eight intersecting lines, identify your eight Ilities in a clockwise order, the most important being at "12 o'clock high". Your team should already have reached agreement on the definition and measurements for these.

Strategic Design Ility "Spider Chart"

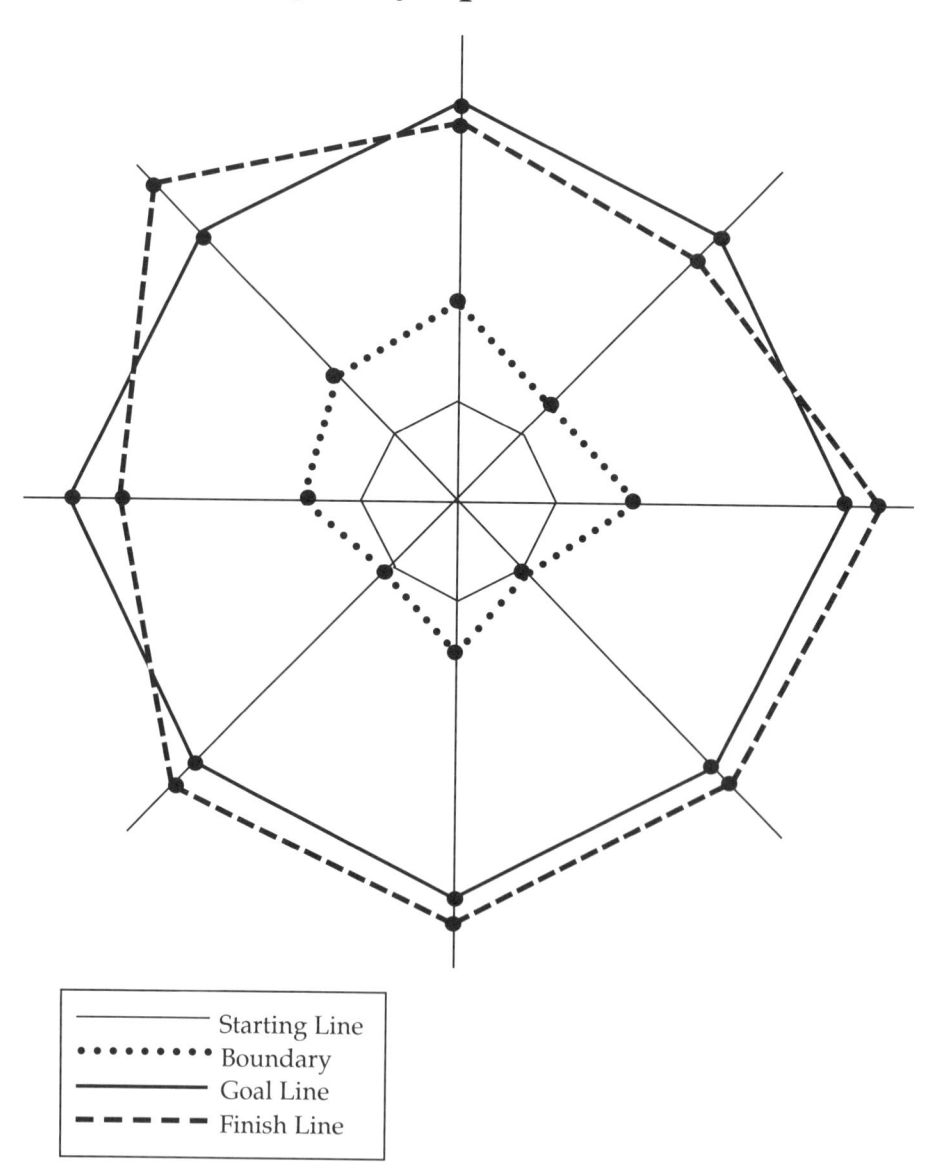

———————	Starting Line
• • • • • • • • •	Boundary
———————	Goal Line
– – – – –	Finish Line

Step Two: Lay in your "goal line"

Draw a large diameter circle to represent your Ility goal line. Sketch in your Ility goal measurements where the circle intersects your Ility lines.

Step Three: Lay in your "starting line"

Good measurement is not only knowing where you want to go, but where you are starting from. For example, you may be in New York and your goal is to go to Los Angeles. You may know the precise quadrants of Los Angeles, but without some knowledge of where you are starting from you could head in entirely the wrong direction.

Likewise with good design, you must make a frank assessment of where you are with each of your Ility starting points.

Draw a smaller diameter circle to represent your design starting points for each Ility. Define each of these starting points using the same measurement you are using for your goal line.

Using our refrigerator compressor example again, the present compressor model requires about 12 minutes installation time. The team wants to achieve installability by reducing this time by 50%.

The distance between your starting line and your goal line is measured as a **percentage of completion.** This commonizes measurements between all 8 Ilities and enables your team to quickly assess trade-offs during your design innovation process.

With some Ilities, you will be working from a higher number to a lower number, such as in the reduction of assembly time. In other cases, you will be working from a lower number to a higher one. For example, this might mean increasing reliability from 15 years Mean Time Between Failure to 20 years MTBF.

Use best judgement when hard data is not available. Remember, this is the concept stage when measurement precision is not important, but direction and strategy selection is. Always remember that your team measurements will be later challenged by management. Be ready to support them.

Step Four: Lay in your "boundary line"

Design boundaries are both external and internal. External boundaries are set, for example, by the customer, the marketplace, and the environment. Internal boundaries are set by your organization, such as profit, capital investment, strategic policies, and others.

In the case of our compressor design team, the customer has clearly told them their new design must be 10% more energy efficient. These boundary points are sketched-in to show the minimum performance the team must achieve.

Step Five: Gain management consensus

Share your Ility chart with management before you use it. Do they agree with your strategy? Are your goals high enough? Are they too high? Is the rank order of importance the best? How does your strategy fit with the organization's overall company strategy?

Never implement a design strategy without first gaining the concurrence of management. The result will be wasted time, weakened morale, and squandered dollars.

The next step, of course, is to use the tool to measure alternate designs. This is done by overlaying the Ility performance of each design iteration. In some cases, designs will go well beyond the goal points.

Each design will have a different finish line you can use to compare alternate solutions.

Both management and design teams favor Ility charts because:

1. **Highly visual.** They can see what is happening with design progress.

2. **Quantitative.** They can track progress numerically.

3. **Comparative.** They can document alternate approaches.

4. **Integrative.** Everybody's voice is heard.

5. **Easily done.** They don't waste valuable design time.

Chapter Summary

In this chapter, you learned how to build a product design strategy and how to rate designs for their competitive performance. You learned a multi-functional team design tool for maximizing your Ilities.

In the next chapter, you will learn how to minimize your Ings, those sometimes unneeded tasks that are the killers of all elegant designs.

Here is a list of ilities to jump start your strategic thinking.

Adaptability	Learnability
Affordability	Manufacturability
Bendability	Packageability
Brazability	Pourability
Checkability	Readability
Compatibility	Recoverability
Deliverability	Recycleability
Designability	Reliability
Disposability	Removeability
Distributeability	Reuseability
Documentability	Serviceability
Flexability	Shipability
Formability	Storeability
Identifiability	Testability
Implantability	Toolability
Imprecisionability	Trackability
Impressability	Transmitability
Injectionability	Transportability
Installability	Understandability
Integratability	Unpackageability

Chapter 8.

Reducing Product Complexity: Minimizing Your Ings

If Ilities are what makes a product great, Ings can spell its downfall.

What are they? **Ings are all the tasks required to create, manufacture, maintain, and dispose of your product.** Ings are the processes, or tasks, which your design sets in motion, beginning at your early design concept stage.

Once you leave the design concept stage, Ings begin to make their appearance with such tasks as detailing, documenting, prototyping, testing, and many more.

As you release your product design, they sprout up on your supplier's floor as well as in your purchasing office with such tasks as specifying, qualifying, manufacturing, inspecting, and shipping and many, many more.

Ings then begin to appear on your own factory floor with such highly visible tasks as manufacturing, assembling, and shipping. But then other Ings, these not so visible, begin to take their toll in time and cost. These include stocking, scheduling, supervising, re-working, packaging, and, once again, many, many more.

We then begin to see that many of these "visible" Ings carry with them the excess baggage of additional "hidden" Ings.

For example, the highly visible task of painting carries with it the requirement for the hidden tasks of special storage of the paint and solvents, environmental protection for both the painter and the external environment, special preparation for the surface to be painted, and then special packaging to protect the painted surface.

Many times the hidden cost is 20-30 times the visible cost of these troublesome ings.

Finally, Ings make their appearance on your customer's floor, as he receives your product. Your customer is burdened with installing, training, servicing, and, finally disposing of your product.

Your primary goal must be to identify and eliminate as many of these life cycle ings as possible in your earliest design stage.

The Ings you select for your design, either knowingly or unknowingly, are the primary drivers of your product's quality, cycle time and total life span cost.

For example, your product's quality is determined, in large part, by the number of types of Ings you specify in your design. Every ing is an opportunity for something to go wrong. Reduce the number of ing tasks and you will significantly improve your quality level.

Motorola learned this with the design of their "Bandit" pager product line. They significantly reduced quality defects by eliminating manufacturing Ing tasks. Fewer manufacturing tasks meant that less process control was required with far fewer steps to potentially fail.

And then there is product cycle time. Time, whether in your design room, on your factory floor, or on your customer's floor, is the sum total of all the time required by your product's Ings. Design smarter by selecting Ings which create less time and you will significantly reduce total product cycle time.

Conventional accounting methods fall short of capturing the cost of all these Ings. Ask your accounting department to help you "estimate the cost of our product design" and you will be given an estimate of only your new product's tangible, visible costs, such as labor and material. Intangible hidden costs are usually lumped into one category called "overhead," or indirect expense and are allocated across product labor hours, a practice which tells you very little about how to reduce these costs by design.

In short, conventional accounting practices help us little to understand real product cost and, in fact, may force us to make bad design decisions. Billions of manufacturing dollars were sent overseas by U.S. companies in the eighties, all in search of lower costs.

Many of these are now returning as manufacturers realize the hidden overhead costs of overseas sourcing. They are now making indirect cost part of their sourcing decision-making, not just direct labor rate dollars.

The advent of Activity Based Costing (ABC), with its unconventional technique of allocating total internal cost to individual product lines, has shed new light on real factory floor costs. But much ABC cost information has been difficult to transfer to the early design stage. ABC tells us a lot about specific product costs but very little about the specific Ing costs of those products. The information is still not yet in a format for helping a product design team assess complete costs.

Concurrent engineering can go a long way in helping your design team understand total life span product costs. Just assembling a multi-functional team means you have in one place all those who truly understand, and even suffer from, these hidden Ing costs.

Your challenge: Despite the lack of "hard" accounting information available at the early design concept stage, you must widen your cost equation to include these hidden costs.

You must also give them guidance for educating others on your team about these hidden costs. You must also give them a way for measuring their influence at your early product design stage.

The best way to do this is to go beyond conventional accounting practice to **understand and measure the root cause driver of all costs — product Ing complexity.** The dollars that eventually show up on an accounting sheet are set in motion by the complexity of tasks required by a product's design. **Reduce the complexity of those tasks, or Ings, and you will be attacking a product's potential for creating both visible and hidden cost.**

There are some Ings which create more trouble — in quality, cycle time and total cost — than others. By especially working on eliminating these, your team will go a long way in reducing cost. These "Seven Evil Ing Families" are summarized at the end of this chapter.

A word of caution about reducing your product's hidden, indirect expense: Don't look for the results to show up immediately. Unlike the visible, direct costs of labor and material, your gains in reducing indirect expense will remain hidden by your accounting department's costing method. But this does not mean you should ignore the opportunity to reduce these costs.

Global Ing Mapping

Here is an easy-to-use tool for getting your design team to understand and attack Ing complexity, the root cause driver of all product cost, both hidden and visible.

Your first task is to make these troublesome Ings visible to your design team. Sketching a Global Ing Map does this. It is a brainstorming tool used by your team to **understand product life span complexity, or Ing tasks.**

A Global Ing Map can be used at any step in the Strategic Design method to better understand the process complexity of your present product, your competitor's product, or your future product.

Step One: Begin by disassembling your first design, an existing one you are trying to improve, or even your competitor's product, into its component parts. Do this disassembly for each one of your product's life span quadrants, i.e., Design, Factory, Supplier, and Customer.

Step Two: Divide your team into smaller groups of experts on each of the four life span quadrants. For example, have your manufacturing members in one group, your designers in another, your sales and marketing in still another. These experts will best understand all of the tasks, or Ings, required by each of these parts or sub-components.

Step Three: Ask each group to consider each part or sub-assembly in turn and brainstorm all the Ings, or tasks, which would be required by each. Set a time goal of no more than one hour. The objective is to surface all the major life span tasks required by a design concept.

Step Four: Re-group your entire team and share what each sub-group has discovered. The goal is to reveal the total life span complexity of the design concept to the entire team. Brainstorm ideas for eliminating the most time-consuming Ings.

In the next chapter, you will learn how you can use such a Global Ing Map as a first step in measuring your design's potential for hidden cost.

Today "process re-engineering" is the latest catch word. This is the notion of mapping processes in place throughout your company and then simplifying and streamlining them to reduce cost. But, in reality, the best place to reduce unneeded process tasks is not by re-engineering, but by eliminating them before they ever see the light of day.

Global Ing Mapping helps your design team do this. Knowing the basic "Rules of Ing" is an absolute necessity for any design team. Here they are:

The Rules of Ing

1. A product's quality, cycle time and life span cost is the sum of its Ings, not a product's assembled parts.
2. "Parts" are nothing more than integrated Ings. They are "Th-Ings". First begin your design effort by eliminating "Things". When you eliminate a "Thing" you achieve a "No-Thing".
3. Fewer "Things" may not result in a better design. But fewer life cycle Ings always will.
4. Your product design sets in motion all life cycle Ings. Try to reach your ility goals using as few Ings as possible.
5. A product's "manufacture-Ings" are typically far less than its total life cycle Ings. Look for Ing reduction where it will give you a competitive advantage, well beyond your factory floor.
6. Don't focus on "reducing cost" at your early design stage. Focus on reducing your design's Ings. They are the "root cause" of all life cycle quality, time and cost.
7. All Ings do not create equal pain. Some Ings create far more quality, time and cost problems than others.
8. The worst Ings are those from the "Seven Evil Families of Ing." These families create the biggest problem today — Hidden Cost. The following chart describes these "families".

The Seven "Evil Families of Ing"

Evil Ings	Clues	Problems
Variability	Difficult to control processes, SPC required to maintain quality level	Inspection, test, rework, scrap
Precision	Tolerances at outer limits of your organization's skill or experience	Costly equipment, tooling, training maintenance, scrap
Complex Architecture	Many inside and outside steps needed to complete a part and its related processes. Failure of one defeats all.	Excessive handling, long cycle time, "in and out" processing, scheduling and tracking costs
Sensitivity	Part easily flawed during factory or post-factory stages.	Special packaging, rework, field service
Immaturity	Use of processes not previously used or unproven for your specific application.	"Learning curve" time, expensive design, test and validation time
Environmental Requirements	Process closely monitored by governmental agencies, detrimental impact on employees or public.	Employee protection, disposal, liability, documentation costs
Skill Intensive	High degree of training required, number of capable employees limited.	Inspection, training, supervision, monitoring

Institute for Competitive Design ©

These seven evil Ing families set in motion most of the expense we know today as "indirect cost," or "overhead." Attacking these evil Ing families which set in motion this indirect cost must be the major objective of your design team.

Chapter Summary

In this chapter, you learned how reduce the number of Ings your design will create during its entire life span. Ings are process steps, or tasks, a product design sets in motion from the first to the last day of its life span. Sketching a Global Ing Map reveals process steps many times missed by a product design team.

Ing complexity is the root cause driver of most quality, cost and time-to-customer. Every Ing presents an opportunity for a task to be done wrong with the result being poor quality. Every Ing takes time and costs money. Applying the "Rules of Ing" to your product design can spell the difference between a product's success — or failure.

In the next chapter, you will learn another "in-process" measurement tool. This tool enables your team to track its efficiency level, enabling them to correct any human dynamics problems before they reach the critical stage.

Chapter 9.

How To Measure Your Team's Efficiency

Design your team process first, that is, how you will organize yourselves. Then go to work on designing your product.

This simple rule can spell the difference between your design team succeeding...or losing.

Poor organizational efficiency defeats more teams than any other single cause. You can muster the greatest talent in the world and still have chaos, confusion, and failure.

I spend a good deal of my time debriefing design teams to learn why they won—and why they lost. Time and time again, organizational dynamics tops the list as the greatest problem. At the bottom of the list is a lack of technical skill.

Some Problems:

Decisions are not made quickly. People are not on time or even miss key meetings. Buy-in is weak with team members not really committed to implementing decisions or even understanding their role in carrying them out. These are the major causes of failure.

There are many excellent books on teamanship. It is not the purpose of this book to duplicate their efforts. But once you have launched your concurrent engineering team, you must continually make sure that they are working at peak efficiency.

The following Strategic Design tool is designed to specifically measure how well a concurrent engineering team is working. It focuses on the seven major drivers of design team efficiency.

The Strategic Design Team Efficiency Measurement Tool is solidly based on the concept of continuous improvement, constantly analyzing how to improve the process of product development.

Using it will help you and your team:

1. Set a standard of team conduct.
2. Surface human dynamics problems early, well before they create serious trouble.
3. Measure how efficiently the team is working.
4. Assure management that your design team is performing at peak power.

Strategic Design Team Efficiency Measurement Tool

Most design teams use this measurement tool at least every 30 days. If there is a serious human dynamics problem, some teams may even use it more frequently.

The entire team is asked to individually rate the efficiency of their team performance. The goal is to measure total team process, not the individual performance of team members.

This evaluation is done "in the blind". Each member has no knowledge of how his fellow team members are rating the team's performance. The purpose of the measurement is to identify and quantify problems so the team can, as a unit, go to work on solving them.

A generic version of this measurement tool, already used by hundreds of design teams, follows below. You should feel free to modify it in any way to suit your team's circumstances. Experience shows, however, that you should not have more than 10 major issues. Here are the ground rules for its use:

Steps In Using The Team Efficiency Tool

Step 1. Copies of the measurement tool are distributed to each team member by the team leader. The entire team discusses each of the seven efficiency measurements (listed on the next page) to make sure they all have the same understanding in mind. The team leader encourages changing words, even the format, to gain team consensus and buy-in for the tool.

Step 2. Each team member privately evaluates total team efficiency on each of the seven points. Using a rating scale of 1-10 (10 is perfect performance), the individual team member scores the team on each issue. If he rates any issue at lower than a 7, he is required to write in, under the comments section, his thoughts on how to correct the problem. No criticism of an individual team member is permitted.

Step 3. A non-team member, someone who preferably does not know team members' handwriting, collates all the responses and records all the written comments. A composite summary is then typed, showing the average ratings for the group, and all comments. This is distributed to all team members to review in private.

Step 4. The leader calls a team meeting to review the results and to brainstorm ideas for improving efficiency performance. The written ideas submitted by team members serve as a jumping off point. Major decision making may even be postponed until a particular human dynamics problem is resolved.

In most cases, the design team sponsor, or upper management person guiding the team, is not included in these evaluation discussions. The primary goal is to build a stronger sense of self-management among the team. Not including management usually enables team members to address issues in a more open, frank manner.

Management should be made aware, however, that your team is actively addressing the issue of team dynamics in a continuous improvement manner. This builds management confidence in your design team's effort.

Strategic Design

Team Efficiency Measurement Tool

The Seven Measurements

1. Involvement Level. Rate how well you feel all team members individually participate in discussion, opinion sharing, etc. Are some team members being left out? Do some members dominate discussion, leaving little time for the voices of all members to be heard? Are some members reluctant to contribute?

1   2   3   4   5   6   7   8   9   10
  (Poor)   (Average)   (Perfect)

Comments:

2. Open-Minded Spirit. Rate how well your team listens to one another. Are all ideas given an open and fair hearing? How well are "way out" concepts welcomed?

1   2   3   4   5   6   7   8   9   10
  (Poor)   (Average)   (Perfect)

Comments:

3. Technical Skill. Rate the technical competence of your team. Are all team members able to keep up with the demands of your design task? Are some skills lacking? Are some skills over-represented?

1   2   3   4   5   6   7   8   9   10
  (Poor)   (Average)   (Perfect)

Comments:

4. Decision-Making. Rate the quality of your team's decision-making. Is there a strong sense of buy in when a decision has been reached? Does everyone participate in the process? Does it move quickly and efficiently? Is consensus decision-making being used for major issues?

1   2   3   4   5   6   7   8   9   10
    (Poor)   (Average)   (Perfect)

Comments:

5. Mutual Respect. Are ideas reviewed and criticized frequently, frankly, and rather comfortably? Are there any signs of personal attack, either openly or in a hidden fashion?

1   2   3   4   5   6   7   8   9   10
    (Poor)   (Average)   (Perfect)

Comments:

6. Organizational Efficiency. Rank your team's ability to plan its work schedule and maintain organizational discipline. Is time being used efficiently?

1   2   3   4   5   6   7   8   9   10
    (Poor)   (Average)   (Perfect)

Comments:

7. Leader/Team Interaction. Is the team hampering the leader's facilitative role or vice versa? Is either one playing too dominant a role?

1 2 3 4 5 6 7 8 9 10
   (Poor)   (Average)   (Perfect)

Comments:

Chapter Summary

In this chapter, you learned the importance of designing your team dynamics before beginning to design your product.

You also learned an in-process measurement tool to periodically measure your team's efficiency level in order to detect any problems before they become major ones.

In the next chapter, you will learn tips and techniques for selecting your concurrent engineering software with minimum pain and confusion. How well you do this will contribute to the overall efficiency of your design effort.

Chapter 10.

How To Select Your Design Software With Less Pain

No task requires more time, intensive effort and sheer agony than the challenge of deciding what software technology to buy for your concurrent engineering effort.

Over the past decade, companies like yours have spent millions on computer-based tools only to discover later that much of this money was wasted.

The manager who spearheaded the selection process is typically singled out as the culprit. He is the one left shouldering most of the blame.

As a good friend of mine confided to me after going through such an experience, "I was left swinging in the wind."

This chapter will help you successfully lead your company to the right decision. You can avoid much mental anguish, and perhaps even a shattered career, by heeding the advice which follows.

Selecting the right engineering software technology tools doesn't require that you be a computer "guru." It does mean, though, that you practice some common sense fundamentals.

How this chapter will help you

This chapter describes the four basic things you must know to guide your company to an intelligent decision. These are:

1. What factors today are driving the new innovations in engineering software design.
2. Why so many companies made wrong decisions in the past.
3. What rules to follow to make your selection successful.
4. How to develop a selection strategy.

This chapter is not intended to give you detailed information on all engineering software available. There is a bewildering array of tools on the marketplace today, all with their own merits.

It is intended to help you make the right decision and avoid damaging your career. You will also find it helpful in educating fellow managers on what they should know about engineering software today.

Factors driving software revolution

Be aware of these four factors driving engineering software innovation. They are the ones which are creating most of the rapid change in the computer-aided design field.

First is the increased pace of product development cycles. Companies today are releasing product improvements sooner in an attempt to outpace their competitors. Cycle time reduction is the battle cry of many today.

Compressing design time not only means beating your competition to market but also using your precious design resources more efficiently.

Another benefit is increasing your learning curve cycles. As one concurrent engineering manager told me, "We get our new products in the field faster to find out sooner how they can be improved for the customer. Continuous improvement is the name of the design game here...not "if it works, don't fix it."

Make sure your software accelerates communication between players on your concurrent engineering team.

Second is that customers are asking for improved product performance, as well as a wider choice in product type.

Product models are proliferating at a rapid pace. Companies are racing to fill niche markets before their competitors discover them. Each new opportunity brings different performance requirements.

> "Our product design software is working overtime to keep up," one manager told me. "Fortunately, it's flexible enough to look at many different design options simultaneously. We can alter designs quickly and painlessly."

Make sure your engineering software doesn't force you to start all over again when a new customer appears on the horizon.

Third is that the quality revolution is now moving upstream from the factory floor to the design room. Managers now recognize that a design's concept drives 70% — or more — of all product quality.

"Up front and right!" is fast becoming more than a slogan. Companies want fewer engineering changes. They want to be sure major performance requirements are going to be met long before prototypes are built.

Make sure your software enables easy performance analysis, "up front" at the concept stage, without hindering communication between members of your design team.

Fourth is that the emergence of concurrent engineering means team members must work simultaneously. Companies are now demanding that all team members have unobstructed access to design models.

Smart managers recognize a computer master model can serve as a focal point for team communication, eliminating confusion. Yet they also realize there must be control in the master model to oversee design integrity. New advances in software now make this "best of both possible worlds" available.

Make sure your software system gives you the same benefits.

Fifth is that software technology is changing at an exponential rate. Features are available today which were only talked about two years ago. The computer-aided design field is becoming fiercely competitive.

Many software suppliers are failing to make the cut, leaving their customers stranded with closed-ended systems. The greatest bottom line cost is the customer's task of starting their learning process again with a new supplier.

Smart companies are now paying more attention to their engineering software supplier's ability to keep up with this technology horse race.

Make sure your supplier has the horsepower to go the long distance. Consider product features but look beyond to your supplier's track record as well as financial statement.

Past failures prologue to future

The key to understanding the future, a wise man once said, is understanding the past. In less than ten years, computer-aided design has moved rapidly from being an "electronic drawing board" to solid modeling to now fully-integrated design, manufacturing, and engineering systems.

CAD (Computer-aided design) is now CAD/CAM/CAE (Computer-aided design, manufacture, and engineering). This engineering software revolution is now in its fourth stage.

Along the way, too many companies paid the price of not recognizing where this change was going. Here is a brief historical synopsis of these stages to make sure you are pointed in the right direction. It is intended to help your keep this software revolution in perspective.

First stage: electronic drawing board

First generation engineering software pitted manual drawing creation against the computer, the pencil against the CAD screen. The measure of performance was speed. Drawing productivity was the primary goal. Success was measured in number of drawings completed in a specified period of time.

"It was the era of the two-dimensional electronic drafting board," an engineering manager told me. "John Henry against the steam powered pile driving machine."

There was no contest. These CAD systems proved faster and more accurate. Like John Henry, the drawing boards were retired, never to be used again.

But the way the design process worked was left unchanged. Some managers began to realize speeding up the drafting did not improve the quality of design.

Tasks were still done in series. Designers designed, analysts analyzed, and test engineers performed test analyses.

Simulation studies, such as failure modes analysis, still required additional models had to be created. This continued to be a cumbersome, time consuming process.

Second stage: 3D solid modeling

In the mid-eighties, the birth of 3D solid modeling began to revolutionize the process of design, the way a design team worked together.

Solid modeling brought visualization, a powerful way for both technical as well as non-technical people to see the design as it was being created. Designers could check for interference fits, and packaging specialists concerned about envelope dimensions could begin working on their design task months ahead.

Now marketing, field-service and even customers could get a vivid feeling for the final product. Their voices began to be heard earlier in the design process, a first step in the movement toward concurrent engineering.

Error-proof drawings could be quickly extracted from these geometry-based solid models.

But some managers continued to be troubled. As one manager who went through this period recalled, "We were told by software vendors we would get better products faster. We got faster designs, but 'better' was questionable."

Many managers began to see that if their new product pushed the old performance envelopes they might end up with the same problems they saw in a manual design, especially if they were working on a tight schedule.

Companies began to ask for more than just fast geometry. They began to demand better quality, plus even more speed.

Third stage: performance design

By the early 90's, software suppliers (those which had survived the brutal competition of the late 80's) began to shift their focus to improving design performance, not just drafting speed. They began to offer software technology for improving the quality of the product up front, not just creating slick-looking geometric models.

FEA became an expected part of a CAD system. Now high performance product designs, from aircraft to power tools, underwent rigorous analysis before design details were complete. Companies could team solid modeling with analysis to produce a better design faster.

But one sticky problem remained. With most software systems, the analysis and design systems did not reside on the same computer workstation. Some were on a common disc, but this didn't mean they could work together.

This lack of integrated analysis created human problems, especially for teams just beginning to experiment with concurrent engineering.

For example, analysis continued to be performed by different people in a different group. Many times most of the solid model geometry had to be recreated for the analysis to be performed.

One frustrated manager summed it up best: "Just when my boss was asking for 'concurrent engineering,' and I need immediate results on the performance of a new design, I'm throwing my CAD model over an electronic fence to some analyst who used different software and who doesn't have a clue what my design is all about."

Fourth stage: no more electronic fences

Engineering software is now in its fourth stage. It is this stage which holds the most promise for your concurrent engineering effort.

Today the electronic fences can be torn down if you make the right engineering software decisions. Some systems are even so well integrated that the CAD design guy and analysis guy can be the same person.

Following is a checklist of eight key rules to help you make the right software decision for your concurrent engineering effort.

- Rule 1. Make sure the computer model you use for analysis is the same CAD model you use for design.
- Rule 2. Make sure your team has a one master model that is up-to-date at all times.
- Rule 3. Make sure you avoid the problems created by multiple software vendors by using a single, integrated system.
- Rule 4. Make sure there is centralized control over design integrity.
- Rule 5. Make sure your software selection is easy-to-use.
- Rule 6. Make sure your system enables your designers to work the way they naturally think.
- Rule 7. Make sure your system offers "optimization," a form of advanced intelligent assistance, and that this is linked directly to your master CAD model.
- Rule 8. Select a reputable software supplier with a proven track record who will be around for the long haul.

Follow these rules

Each of these eight key rules are explained below. Following them will help you avoid the painful experience of learning only too late that you and your company have stumbled in your choice of software systems.

> **Rule 1. Make sure the computer model you use for analysis is the same one you use for design.**

Don't buy a system with electronic fences built in. The best systems have an architecture which makes your analysis integral with your design. The analysis tools are imbedded in the design code. The designer builds design geometry and analytical geometry in the same software, using the same commands.

Gone are the days when you have to wait for a new model to be created for your analysis engineers. In the 80's, it was first thought that if you link a CAD system to a third party analysis tool, you could easily perform all the analytical tasks you needed. But hard experience showed this was far from a simple task.

What most of the links from design models to third party analysis software actually do is to transfer only basic geometry. Linking codes is still a tricky task. Only part of your data may be transferred.

Many times, the designer is faced with developing a new model, with time for analysis. He may even have to re-create much of the geometry that wasn't transferred by the data link.

> **Rule 2. Make sure your team has one master model that is up-to-date at all times.**

Chose a system that allows you to create one model from which all your team members can derive the information they need.

Look for a system which gives your team the capability of performing analysis on the master design model. This helps you avoid the problems of going to a different model or a different code. It all resides together.

For example, if your analysis engineer suggests a change in your design, the FEA model is changed on the spot. Communication problems are avoided. Your designer uses the same commands he has learned for solid modeling and drafting.

The change merely updates the master model. There is no need for an analyst. The designer becomes the analyst.

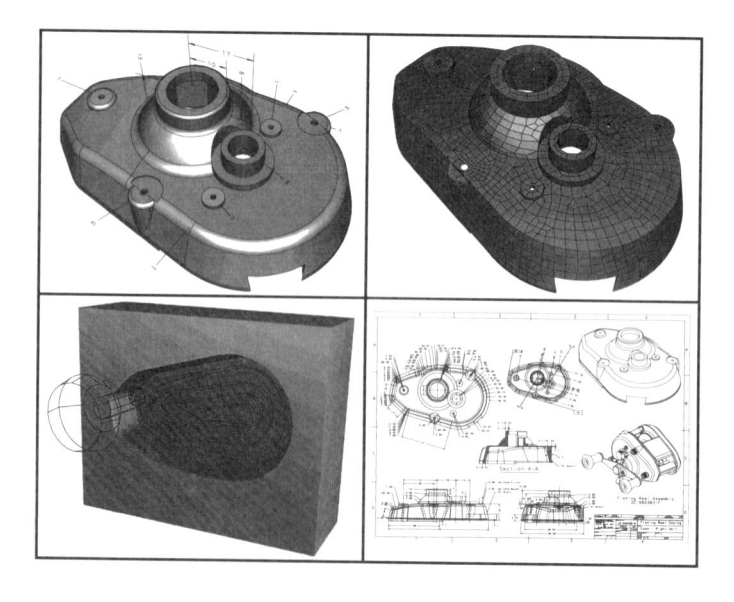

Choose a single integrated software system which allows you to easily move between design, analysis, machining, and drafting applications. I-DEAS Master Series™ photo courtesy of SDRC.

Rule 3. Make sure you avoid the problems created by multiple suppliers by using a single, integrated system.

Look for a system which enables you to perform analysis using one integrated system. This means you don't have to go to a different supplier's code or a different model.

Linking design with third party analysis codes means you must also keep a close eye on the integrity of the link. You may find that one of your vendors might make a change in code or operating systems and render your link inoperable.

Business relationships also change. A link developed today between two companies' software products may dissolve in a few years, temporarily crippling your design capability.

Rule 4. Make sure there is centralized control over design integrity.

Clearly understand the difference between "concurrent associativity" and "bi-directional associativity" before you make your software choice. Knowing what these tongue-twisters mean is important for maintaining the integrity of your design.

Bi-directional associativity means anyone who has access to your model can make any changes they like. No control is provided in the master, or base model, to oversee design integrity. As one frustrated project manager complained to me, "The last one to make a change wins!"

For example, a draftsman could make an innocent — but wrong — design change with good intentions and it will be incorporated for all future use. Project release management can become a nightmare as there is no central control of design updates.

Design changes are automatically forced on drawings, assemblies, and even NC tool paths. There is no choice.

Systems with bi-directional associativity limit the extent data can be shared simultaneously. This means multiple copies of the data must be created. And this can lead to flawed design integrity when user discipline lags, as it inevitably does.

Concurrent associativity is by far the best approach. Only one user is permitted to check-out, modify, and check-in a master model at a given time. Other users can concurrently "reference" the design during this same period but the system prevents them from modifying the design at their own will.

For example, an analysis design engineer can check-out the latest design version to conduct application studies but could not modify the master model.

Design changes can only be made by authorized team members, thus maintaining the integrity of your master model.

As a concurrent engineering manager, it is important that the system you select solves the two major problems of a team sharing a design model: (1) Master model access and control and (2) Model updates and change notification.

Concurrent associativity solves both of these for you. It enables your team members to focus on their individual tasks, while your master model is constantly refined in a disciplined, step-by-step manner.

All team members are alerted to changes in the master version, can see the impact on their own work and can update their work automatically should they chose to do so.

Rule 5. Make sure your software is easy-to-use, both for modeling and analysis.

Early computer-aided design analysis was complex and required far more training than most CAD tools. This tended to create a "team within a team" of specialists, making it difficult for the entire design group to know in what direction their design was moving.

Today much has been done to take the mystery out of design analysis, making such tasks easier for all product engineers.

This has also boosted a greater degree of design understanding and ownership.

Look for systems which include on-line expert systems to help your team through their analysis tasks. These are usually developed from the combined experience of seasoned analysts who have performed similar tasks for many years.

Benefits for you include less up-front training, faster usage of the software, and less re-training. This is especially true for complex analysis tasks which are far more difficult to remember.

For example, SDRC now offers a "simulation advisor" for leading designers through all analysis steps from modeling to final review of results. This feature works as an intelligent user interface, continually providing advice on best practices for the task being done.

Very importantly, this simulation advisor can be customized by you in order to imbed your company practices, or protocols, into the system.

Rule 6. Make sure your system helps your designers work the way they normally think.

Look for systems that enable your designers to work the way they naturally think. These are called "intuitive" systems.

Avoid systems which require your design teams to pre-define part parameters when first describing the part to the CAD system. These "parametric modeling" systems require your designers to anticipate all aspects of the part they are designing, as well as those features they may want to change later.

This is not how designers intuitively work and too often results in re-configuring the part from the ground up. As one project manager commented to me, "Using parametric modeling sometimes forced us to hit a brick wall and then start all over again."

Intuitive, or flexible, modeling systems give your designers more freedom. They design the way they think. Flexible modeling allows design changes or alterations to be accommodated quickly and painlessly. It dismantles the brick wall.

Rule 7. Make sure your system offers "optimization," a form of advanced intelligent assistance.

New software systems now feature an advanced form of intelligent assistance called *optimization*. This is a feature to help your designers develop the correct geometry to achieve the best, or optimum, product condition, be it weight, minimum stress, or maximum stiffness.

The first use of optimization focused on sizing structures using shell and beam finite element representations to solve basic engineering problems. For example, the software system could quickly review 40-50 design variables to show significant design improvement in only 3-4 design iterations.

Today, these capabilities have grown to include such features as general sensitivity analysis and shape re-design based on finite element node movement.

More important, this optimization is now directly linked to the master design model geometry. This means your team can design for minimizing mass, stress or deflection while staying within stress, deflection and natural frequency constraints and still update the dimensions of your solid model.

Rule 8. Select a reputable software supplier with a proven track record who will be around for the long haul.

This is the most important rule of all. The greatest cost of software technology is your *internal integration*, or your company's learning curve cost, not the initial purchase price.

Select a supplier who goes out of business and you will be faced with a major re-learning project.

Or choose a supplier who is unwilling or unable to aggressively improve the technology of their software, and you will fall behind your competitors.

Or select a software technology which is not flexible enough to grow and you may "dead end."

Look beyond your potential supplier's product to understand his software development process. How much is he spending for research and development? Is he involving customers like yourself to make sure his technology is serving their real needs? Is his software technology structured to allow flexibility and growth?

Make sure you select a supplier who will be around for the long haul, has the technical expertise to grow with you, and offers a software which doesn't drive you down a dead end.

Your Selection Strategy Checklist

There is no software available today that will please everyone in your company. And the software technology that will completely meet all your concurrent engineering needs is yet to be written.

But there are some basic steps to help you chose a software technology that will go the farthest in meeting these two goals.

My advice to you is based on a single, fundamental fact:
Selecting software is easy, integrating it is difficult.

Make sure your selection process involves all those who must integrate the software into their daily working lives. Make your users the real owners of your company's final decision by gaining their buy-in from the start of the selection process.

Here is a step-by-step checklist for making sure you are on the right track.

1. Form a multi-functional selection team.

Include both managers and hands-on users. Make sure all departments are involved, including marketing, field service, and others who may not enter data but will have to understand the output of the system. The major mistake of the past was to include too few, not too many, departments.

Make sure your team members clearly understand they will play the major role in making the final decision, not you. Your role should be that of a facilitator.

Absolutely make sure you include your major suppliers early in the process. They will have to use the output of your software technology. They can also be a good source of information on the latest software technology available.

The best team structure is a core team of 4-6 with a second ring of team members who interface with the core team only when their expertise is required. The goal should be to minimize meeting time. However, major decisions should be made by the combined team, both core and second ring.

I have found this approach to work well with both a software selection team and a concurrent engineering team.

2. Poll the troops.

Involve your hands-on users from the start. Gather multi-functional groups together for open discussion. Ask them what they do — and don't — like about your current software technology. Get specific. Develop an "internal benchmarking" list of key features you feel your new system should offer. Share with them what you mean by each.

Then divide the meeting into smaller groups and have them brainstorm other features that could be added to the list. Ask each group to report out on their results and add their features to your list.

End the meeting by asking them to (1) Rate how well your present system meets each feature and (2) Rank and weight each feature.

Publish these reports for all to read and understand. Begin to get everyone to agree on what the problems are of the present and where they want to go in the future. Make sure your company has a clear understanding of its software technology problems before your team begins to help solve them.

Remember that software selection is easy, implementation is difficult. You will be measured on your implementation success. Make sure those who will implement it — your hands-on users, fellow managers, and others — see themselves as owners of both the decision and your new software.

3. Invite software suppliers in to educate you.

Invite software technology suppliers in to brief you on where they stand with their latest developments. Don't make any assumptions on where each is with their technology today. Major suppliers are continually upgrading their technology.

Remember to ask them for their user list. Especially ask for the names of companies in your same industry. Begin building a list of companies to benchmark.

4. Benchmark other companies.

Try to visit companies in industries similar to yours. Their software technology needs will parallel yours.

Use your internal benchmarking results to develop a checklist. Ask your external benchmarking partner to rate his software against your list.

Remember to ask them about their own software selection process. Some may be able to give you valuable "tips" to help you guide your own.

Consolidate these results for reporting out to your entire selection team, management, and all users.

5. Educate and involve senior management.

Keep senior management informed. They will be more concerned about your *process* of selection than the software product features you have identified. Try to surface any concerns they may have as early in the selection process as possible.

Report out to them the results of your internal benchmarking, supplier meetings, and external benchmarking efforts. Make sure your entire selection team is on hand to answer any questions. This will help assure them "all voices are being heard."

6. Customize your set of requirements and make sure the troops approve.

Work with your multi-functional team to reduce your company's needs to a final set of requirements. Remember that no software supplier may be able to meet all of them.

What you are interested in is the optimum system for your needs.

Set up a rating system with relative weights for each software feature using the information you gained from your internal benchmarking effort. Then publish this rating system and ask for final comments. Remember to remind everyone about the process you used to build the requirements list.

7. Invite software suppliers to respond to your requirements.

Ask them to show how their product responds to your needs in a step-by-step manner. Ask them for a trial copy of their product for your own internal evaluation.

Have your selection team gain hands-on experience and ask each to report out their findings, using your requirements, ratings and weights for their results.

Avoid random test drives. These usually favor the "easy-to-use" systems but have little to do with your overall, long-range requirements.

Consolidate your selection team results into a final report.

8. Make your decision based on the big picture.

Remind all your selection team members that your goal is a *consensus decision*. Tell them up front there is no software that will meet all the needs of everyone on the team.

Clearly explain to them that a consensus decision is one that everyone agrees to support, not one they feel is the ideal solution. Try to avoid balloting. This may get fast decision-making on all your software features, but it does little for building implementation support.

Ask each team member to individually rate each supplier on each of the features on your requirements list. Ask them to do this prior to your final selection meeting.

Begin your final selection meeting by asking each team member to report out their ratings for each feature. Discuss each in turn until you can reach a consensus on which supplier's product performs best.

The best approach is to have the team member having the lowest, or highest rating, begin the discussion. If you find consensus is difficult, move on to another feature.

Discuss each feature and supplier until you can reach a final consensus decision. Inform senior management and ask for their support. Remember sharing with them the *decision process* your team used to arrive at their choice.

9. Stay involved with your supplier.

Once you have selected a supplier, ask to sit on his customer advisory council. This will give you a chance to network with other users. It will also keep you up-to-date on your supplier's latest improvements.

Chapter Summary

Selecting the wrong software technology for your concurrent engineering effort can spell disaster, both for your company and you as a manager.

This chapter guides you through this difficult task by:

1. Telling you what factors are driving new innovations in engineering software design and why.
2. Giving you the reasons why so many companies made wrong software decisions in the past.
3. Giving you eight rules to follow in making the right selection.
4. Telling you how to develop a winning selection strategy.

In the next chapter, you will learn how to design a company-wide effort to implement concurrent engineering. The techniques and tools described are based on the lessons learned by hundreds of company concurrent engineering facilitators, team leaders, and managers.

Chapter 11.

Spreading The Word: How To Implement Concurrent Engineering Company-Wide

I have yet to meet a concurrent engineering champion who wasn't frustrated by the lack of step-by-step instruction in how to make the process function well in their company.

Much has been written about the "why" of concurrent engineering. Little has been written about the "how to".

The earlier chapters in this book gave you a team design map, tools and measurements. This chapter will give you a step-by-step plan you can use to implement the process company-wide.

All concurrent engineering rollout efforts are different. That is why you may want to modify the following plan to suit your company's unique culture and product line.

But always keep this in mind: At some point or another, you must complete each of the following five steps. Not to do so will, sooner or later, endanger your implementation effort.

Implementing Concurrent Engineering Company-Wide: The Five Key Phases

You must immediately begin to educate and, most importantly, involve three major groups in your company. They are:

Senior Management. Too often senior managers don't clearly understand that concurrent engineering requires a fundamental culture change. Few managers realize that for every one success story they read about in the business press, there are ten concurrent engineering efforts that failed to meet expectations. They see it merely as another tool, easily taught and then applied. This attitude, unless changed, can be dangerous to the career of the person tasked to implement the process.

You must immediately begin to educate senior managers about the difficulty of making the process work. You must also give them a role in your implementation plan. Too often, senior management buys into the process but fails to "walk the talk."

Middle Management. Middle managers are often accused of torpedoing concurrent engineering efforts. Afraid of losing control, they are seen as digging in their heels and resisting the transition to this kind of product design.

While I have sometimes found this to be the case, I now believe that most middle managers fundamentally support the process. I find that the primary reason why they do not energetically support the process is that **no one has defined their new role for them.** Part of your job must be to help them shape this new role.

The Performers. These are members of the design team who will eventually do the "hands on" work. They are also the people who may not be on the design team, but must support their effort. You must make sure that they fully understand the full dimensions of concurrent engineering. This kind of design process requires more work and far more personal responsibility than traditional design.

Not surprisingly, the idea of more work and responsibility doesn't sit well with some people. These are the ones you don't want on your design team, especially your first pilot effort.

The following five phases are intended to both educate and involve these three key groups. This rollout template has already be used by dozens of successful concurrent engineering champions.

Roll-Out Phase I. Sell From The Top Down

1. Re-define the process for top management.

Give your most senior management a **one hour briefing** on the real dimensions and problems of implementing concurrent engineering. If you have attended an Institute for Competitive Design (ICD) Concurrent Engineering

Workshop, use this meeting as the format for reporting out what you have learned. Use Chapters 1-2 of this book as the basis for your presentation. Contact ICD for other free presentation materials.

Show how concurrent engineering helps existing company initiatives such as total quality management, continuous improvement and others.

Clearly explain that concurrent engineering is not another "program of the month" but a process for helping existing efforts work even better. Gain their support for writing your own in-company "Concurrent Engineering User's Guide". (See Chapter 12 in this book for how to do this.)

Gain their support for giving a similar presentation to the users, your fellow employees who will have to understand the process and make it work.

2. Inform (and listen to) the troops.

Conduct a "Concurrent Engineering User's Overview" for those who will eventually serve on design teams.

Modify your management briefing to address the questions users will likely ask. At the end of your briefing conduct an ICD benchmarking exercise to find where they think your company is at in transitioning to this kind of design. (Contact ICD for a copy of the benchmarking tool.) Close your briefing by asking for their written questions about how to make concurrent engineering work in your company environment. You will later use these questions, with answers, in preparing your "User's Guide."

Broaden their understanding as well as begin to identify the "users" major concerns, which you must eventually begin to address. Gain benchmarking data for shaping your implementation strategy, as well as reporting out to management.

Roll-Out Phase II. Develop Your Strategy

1. Identify key goals for your implementation effort.

Using your benchmarking information, identify key goals for your implementation effort, as well as a way of measuring progress in reaching each. Develop the first outline of your implementation plan for Senior Management approval.

Limit the scope of your implementation effort. Focus it on real company problems as defined by the people who have to make the process work.

2. Begin to educate and involve middle management.

Conduct a briefing for middle managers. Ask them to participate in a benchmarking exercise, similar to that done by your users. Then share with them the results of your users benchmarking exercise. Conclude session by asking them to write their "how to" questions.

Begin to gain middle management understanding and buy-in. Deepen your understanding of middle management's implementation concerns.

3. Brief senior management on your benchmarking results.

Using the benchmarking information gained at both your users and middle management sessions, brief senior management on how employees feel about your product delivery process. But before revealing results, have these senior managers take the same benchmarking exercise. You will usually see a similarity between all three, with the senior managers usually being the most optimistic of the groups.

Also share with them the "how" to questions asked by both groups. Give them preliminary answers used by other companies. (See Chapter 12 for the most common questions asked.) Share with senior management your preliminary implementation plan. Request to form a multi-functional "Concurrent Engineering Task Team" composed of key middle managers to act as your advisory group.

Roll-Out Phase III. Innovate Solutions With Users & Management

1. Form a Management Concurrent Engineering Task Team.

Try to make your Task Team as multi-functional as possible. Include naysayers, those who may be directly opposed to this new kind of design. The idea is to make those who may be part of the problem now part of the solution.

As their first task, ask them to review the preliminary draft of your User's Guide. Ask to especially review your section on a functional manager's new role in leading process change, not managing design teams.

2. Select a Pilot Design Project.

Working with your Task Team, select a pilot project for your first concurrent engineering effort.

Follow these tips:

- Make sure it is a meaningful design effort, one which will have a high impact.
- Make sure it has senior management's total support.
- Select one with a short turn around, in which initial results can be visible within one year.

- Select one which is solvable, where some solutions may already be in sight.
- Choose one which does not overly strain existing company resources.

3. Design your team pilot training.

Develop a three-day hands-on workshop for your first team, as well as support staff. Practice just-in-time training, and link the training to the start of your pilot project. This gives you an immediate return on your training investment. Train them in the Strategic Design Method. (See Chapters 3-5). This will assure they are using the concurrent engineering process to its full benefit. Review with the team other design tools such as Quality Function Deployment (QFD), Design of Experiments (DOE) and others. Let them decide which tools best fit their design effort.

Conduct your training in a simulated concurrent engineering environment. Use the Strategic Design Method to first practice on an existing product to better understand past problems. (Contact ICD for training outlines you can use to shape your own effort.) Make sure you distribute an evaluation form at the end of the training session. This will be invaluable in improving your training format.

4. Develop a training program for management.

Conduct a one-day training session for middle managers who must manage in this new design environment. Make this a hands-on session using the Strategic Design Method as the learning focus. Wrap up the session by asking the managers to give written answers to the questions asked by their employees on how to make the process work.

Roll-Out Phase IV. Measure Results.

1. Measure product quality, time, and life cycle performance in early design stages.

Make sure your pilot team is measuring in-process all their key Ilities using the Strategic Design Measurement Chart technique. (See Chapter 7).

Document results using the measurements developed in step two of the Strategic Design Method. As the first Design Brief is completed, make sure your Task Team, as well as senior management, buys into the team's strategic plan.

2. Measure how well the concurrent design process is working company wide.

As the design effort progresses, re-benchmark to see how well the two original groups feel the team and the company is overcoming the problems surfaced in the first benchmarking exercise.

Report these results to management.

3. Ask your team to continuously measure their team efficiency.

Using the Strategic Design Team Efficiency Tool described in Chapter 9, ask your team to continuously track their human dynamics. This builds management confidence in how well the team is working, as well as will surface problems early.

4. Ask your team to be prepared to report out on their "lessons learned" at the end of their design effort.

Ask them for two deliverables. The first is a great design. The second is their advice on what worked, as well as what didn't work. This will be invaluable in helping you continue to improve your implementation effort.

Roll-Out Phase V. Take Continuous Action — Re-Enforce Process Company-Wide.

1. Never stop selling.

As your pilot team, as well as future teams, complete their design efforts, take the time to have them report out to both senior management and the rest of the company. Consider having interchanges between separate design teams and team leaders to share lessons learned.

2. Use your measurement of early design results to build greater buy-in.

Numbers talk. Use the measurements developed with the Strategic Design Method to build greater buy-in.

3. Continually work for company-wide authorship and ownership.

Use the lessons learned by the pilot team to expand your User's Guide. Continue to emphasize that the User's Guide is owned by all and is a working document.

4. Reward the winners.

Make sure to reward winning teams as a group. This encourages team co-ownership. Recognition rewards continue to be the most successful technique used today. Describe the efforts of winning teams in your constantly expanding User's Guide.

Chapter Summary

In this chapter, you learned a step-by-step method for implementing concurrent engineering company-wide. The lessons learned by other facilitators will help you avoid many of their mistakes.

In the next chapter, you will learn how to write your own, customized "Concurrent Engineering User's Guide. A User's Guide gives practical guidance to those who must practice concurrent design.

Chapter 12.

How To Write Your Own Company User's Guide

Concurrent engineering just doesn't come naturally. Not only must you give your company a new design methodology, such as the Strategic Design Method described in previous chapters, you must also provide step-by-step guidance in how to make the process work company-wide.

That is why you must write your own internal Concurrent Engineering User's Guide. Such a guide begins to help design teams, middle management and senior executives answer their sometimes tough how to questions.

This chapter describes a template for such a User's Guide and tips on how to development a successful one. The template shown is a condensed version of one designed by my company, ICD, over the past ten years.

It contains not only step-by-step advice but also examples of the kinds of implementation questions your company will ask. Your goal must be to be able to help others answer such questions.

User's Guide, Not a Policy Book

Your User's Guide should not be written as a corporate policy book. Your role as a company concurrent engineering facilitator is not to write policy. It must be written as a continuously evolving handbook on how a team or management may want to respond to a problem.

In my early days of helping to implement concurrent engineering, I had the mistaken notion that it was management's responsibility to write just how to implement concurrent engineering. I no longer believe that. Too many management policy books are now gathering dust.

I now believe in what I call "ownership by authorship." This is the idea that the people who know how to implement concurrent design best are the ones who will have to use it. In short, the users. And if they have a major hand in preparing their own User's Guide, they will both understand it and use it.

The technique I now recommend is that the facilitator, in cooperation with his management task team, develop a rough draft of a User's Guide, using the following template. "How to" questions, specific to your company, are then gathered from management and design teams.

Using these questions, with answers, customizes the User's Guide for your company's environment.

How To Answer User Questions

Examples of how to answer questions are shown in the following User's Guide template. Note that first a general principle is stated, followed by examples of how other companies have resolved the issue.

Never try to provide a "100% complete" answer. Most of the questions you will be asked have many answers. And all are problem specific. Your goal must be to provide guidance, with your questioner, in cooperation with his team, sponsor or management, answering the rest.

The following User's guide template is for an imaginary company, Acme Corporation. This template is an abbreviated version. Some questions you will be typically asked about concurrent engineering are intentionally given without answers. I have done this to give you a chance to try your hand. All the material you need to answer them is in the User's Guide. For a complete version of this User's Guide, now available in electronic form, contact ICD.

Acme Corporation Concurrent Engineering User's Guide

Contents

I. **How This User's Guide Will Help You**

   [ ] Why Acme needs Concurrent Engineering
   [ ] The 110 Authors
   [ ] When you should use this Guide
   [ ] Why this Guide is not Cast In Stone
   [ ] Your Responsibility For Improving This Guide

II. **Benefits You Can Expect from Concurrent Engineering**

   [ ] Better Quality Up Front
   [ ] Lower Life Cycle Cost
   [ ] Shorter Product Delivery Time
   [ ] Cross-Training
   [ ] Stronger Commitment

III. **The Six Most Common Causes of Failure**

   [ ] Inertia
   [ ] Wrong Measurements
   [ ] Wrong Players
   [ ] Wrong Tools
   [ ] Starting Late
   [ ] Not enough training, coaching & practice

IV. **Common Sense Fundamentals You Must Know**

   [ ] Focus on the enterprise, not its parts
   [ ] Empower those who suffer from design problems most to help solve them
   [ ] Design drives 70% — or more — of all quality, time, and cost
   [ ] Begin early
   [ ] Enlist functional management
   [ ] Understand a problem before you begin to solve it
   [ ] See the big picture
   [ ] Design your team process before you begin your product design
   [ ] Harness the power of peer support
   [ ] Involve management at every step
   [ ] Measure...measure...measure

V. **Your Seven Design Team Tasks and Questions You Will Be Asked Most**

   [ ] Empowering
   [ ] Staffing
   [ ] Leading
   [ ] Organizing
   [ ] Measuring
   [ ] Motivating
   [ ] Leveraging

VI. **Acme Lessons Learned**

   [ ] Valuable experiences from previous design efforts

Section I.

How This User's Guide Will Help You.

This User's Guide will answer your questions on how to make concurrent engineering really work. The fundamentals, guidelines and tips you will read are based on years of experience in solving design team problems.

But the most valuable advice you will receive comes from the experiences of your fellow employees who are already helping to make concurrent engineering work at Acme.

This User's Guide captures these key experiences so that you and your team can benefit from these lessons learned.

Unfortunately, there is no one cookbook solution for assuring that concurrent engineering works every time. Each design challenge is unique. In addition, Acme's design problems are also unique and many times require solutions different from other industries and companies.

There are, however, fundamentals common to all concurrent engineering implementation efforts. This User's Guide will give you these fundamentals as well as answer questions specific to Acme.

Why Acme Urgently Needs Concurrent Engineering Now

Today Acme faces the greatest challenge in its history. Competition in our industry is tough — and getting tougher. Competitors are introducing new product features faster than ever before. And cost is now a major marketing issue.

Concurrent engineering, correctly implemented, can shorten total design time, eliminate costly changes on the manufacturing floor, and improve Acme quality up front.

Our new products must be designed faster, with fewer engineering changes, and at less cost than any previous Acme product effort. While our old design methods may have worked well in the past, today they are incapable of meeting this kind of challenge. What is needed is a re-thinking of our entire design process to put the emphasis on designing right from the start.

Concurrent engineering will help us streamline our product development process.

What Concurrent Engineering Really Is

Concurrent engineering is far more than just multi-functional teams working in co-location. Acme has used multi-functional teams successfully in the past. Many of these designs efforts were also co-located.

Concurrent engineering goes well beyond traditional team design. It requires that all product life cycle problems be addressed, including such issues as manufacturability, serviceability, as well as all the other Ilities.

It requires that the design equation not only include technical factors but hard-headed business factors as well. Concurrent engineering gives far more empowerment to far more people at lower levels in Acme to solve the problems they understand best.

This Guide's Authors

Every Concurrent engineering effort brings a unique set of problems. As part of the preparation for this User's Guide, Acme employees were asked for their questions on implementing this process.

Some (insert number of question) questions were asked, ranging from "Who should be on the design team?" to "How will we measure results?"

These questions provided the direction for writing this User's Guide. It is specifically prepared for the Acme culture and answers the problems most frequently asked by our own people.

How To Use This Guide

You need not read this User's Guide from cover-to-cover to gain a benefit from it. Some of the fundamentals you may already know. (However, it is a good idea to scan them to see if they match with your own). As a team member, you may want only to focus on those sections that directly apply to you.

This User's Guide is designed as a handy reference source. For example, when you are stuck on the problem of motivating your design team, turn to Section IV (Motivating) for some answers.

If you are a newcomer to Concurrent Engineering, read Sections I-IV to give yourself an overall perspective. Then read the Seven Design Team Tasks in Section V on an as needed basis.

Section VI gives you valuable Lessons Learned by previous Acme Concurrent Engineering teams.

Why This Guide Is Not Cast In Stone

There is no "one size fits all" way to implement Concurrent Engineering. That is why this User's Guide is *not a set of policies and procedures*. It is a set of fundamentals with some examples of solutions which have worked well in the past.

This Guide will give you 60-70% of the answers you need. It is up to you and your team to supply the balance of the answer. Also remember that there are no black and white solutions. Every problem has unique factors which directly influence how it should be answered.

Your Responsibility For Continually Improving This User's Guide

Every Concurrent engineering team at Acme has two responsibilities. The first is to deliver a successful design. The second is to improve the process of *how* we design. The key to staying ahead of our competition is a fast, efficient "heads up" design process.

The lessons learned in Section VI of this User's Guide came from the previous experiences of other Acme teams. Your responsibility is to add to these lessons learned with you own experiences and recommendations.

This User's Guide is a living document. You will be called upon to make suggestions for improving it both during, as well as after, your design effort.

Section II.

Benefits You Can Expect From Concurrent Engineering

Design drives 70% — or more — of all product quality, cost and delivery time. While efforts to improve quality and reduce cost on the factory floor are extremely valuable, it is *how we design a product where the greatest gains can be made.*

Concurrent engineering solves more than technical problems. When correctly understood and implemented, it goes beyond conventional engineering problem solving to enable a design team to understand real world business issues.

This process recognizes that the biggest problem facing design teams isn't innovation *but implementation.* Acme has excellent talent for solving (your product line) technical problems. What is urgently required is the more efficient use of this talent with fewer re-starts, changes, and overall design waste.

Concurrent Engineering helps a design team implement technical solutions faster, in less time and with better quality. As one Acme employee commented, "It will help design systems better, quicker, and cheaper."

Better Quality Up Front

Quality must begin on the drawing board. While factory-floor quality improvement solutions are paying off, the best place to cure a quality problem is at the design stage.

Techniques such as Statistical Process Control (SPC) can help control difficult process in the manufacturing area. But the best solution is to minimize the use of these processes at the design stage, or eliminate them altogether.

The manufacturing lessons learned must be moved up to the early design stage, so that they are not repeated. Doing this requires that manufacturing and quality improvement people participate in a *pro-active way* at the early design stage.

This User's Guide will give you insights into new methods for designing quality in up front.

Lower Life Cycle Cost

Conventional design often focuses too closely on factory labor and material cost. But from the Acme customer standpoint, this delivered cost is only the beginning of his real life cycle cost problem.

Life cycle cost includes everything from non-recurring design cost to field maintenance cost and, finally, disposal costs.

Fielding a multi-functional design team which understands all these costs is the first step in identifying and attacking these costs.

Many life cycle costs are hidden. Highly visible costs, for example, are the cost of recurring manufacturing material or components. Another example is manufacturing touch labor, the cost of assembling a (your product line) on the manufacturing floor.

Conventional accounting methods do an excellent job of capturing these kinds of direct cost. Experience and historical cost can help the design team estimate the cost of one design strategy versus another.

Hidden costs are those which design teams find difficult to incorporate into their design decisions. Accounting data does not capture these costs in a way which helps the design team relate them to early design decisions.

Hidden costs are almost endless. They begin appearing with the first day of the design effort and don't end until the product reaches the end of its life cycle.

Examples of hidden cost include wasted design time, manufacturing floor non-value added labor, and unneeded field warranty and service cost. Most times these kinds of costs are pooled and allocated over labor hours and material as a burden factor or indirect expense.

In our industry, these kinds of hidden costs can account for more than 30-50% of a product's in-company cost...or even more. And these percentages do not include post-factory life cycle cost.

Concurrent engineering can attack all costs up front when the design team is properly staffed and the right design methodology used. Downstream employees who clearly suffer from these kinds of hidden costs join the design team early to educate the product designers.

These process owners are trained and challenged to relate their design pain to specific features in current product designs. They are then challenged, working with the technical designers, to find a way to eliminate such pain right from the start.

This User's Guide, as well as the training you will receive with it, will show you and your team how to attack all life cycle cost right from the start.

Shorter Product Delivery Time

The primary goal of all concurrent engineering teams must be to reduce their total product design delivery time. Today, time-to-market can spell the difference between success or failure.

A technically superior design which misses a market window or exceeds development budgets, is a failure which could spell death for the entire enterprise.

Concurrent engineering is flexible. The team works first to clearly understand the dimensions of the total design task. The team then designs itself to complete the task in the most efficient way possible.

Design teams are challenged not only to develop a technically superior design, but to do so in less time.

For example, the design team looks at both schedule and alternate design solutions to decide which solution makes the most sense on a total (your product line) basis.

This may mean some design tasks increase, while others shrink. For example, more time may be spent up front resolving manufacturing issues and communicating procedures better with each drawing.

This strategy may lengthen the design detail stage but will significantly shrink total product development time. It helps limit the multiplier effect of finding manufacturing problems late in the development cycle, or worse when the (your product) is in service.

The goal always must be to maximize the sum of the effort, not merely minimize each functional effort.

Cross-Training

Concurrent engineering can build a stronger, more efficient Acme organization. Cross training is a natural outcome of a well-working design team.

For example, successful design teams quickly recognize that concurrent design can stretch technical resources to the limit. They adopt techniques for reducing meeting time, making decisions more quickly, and developing communication techniques to sharply reduce a technician's input time.

The design team continually improves its team process by having full-time, or core members, become more multi-functional through on-the-job cross-training.

Less demanding technical tasks can be transferred to other team members, freeing up technical experts for more demanding work. Technical experts become more efficient in the use of their time.

"Fewer parts, with each part more multi-functional" is a tenant of good mechanical design. The same holds true for a concurrent engineering team: "Fewer team members, but each cross-trained with more multi-functional skill."

Concurrent engineering provides fertile ground for cross-training.

Stronger Commitment

Successful concurrent engineering requires total team buy in at the early design stage. Each member must have a sense of owning the total design, not just his or her technical piece of the pie.

This total commitment begins early in the design effort with all process owners contributing in defining the design problem. It continues with all major decisions being subjected to the consensus of the team.

The Concurrent Engineering process is strengthened with management *rewarding team success*, not only individual performance. Measurements and rewards are focused on enterprise-wide success, not just departmental performance.

Empowerment to recognize problems early and find innovative ways to fix them is driven down to the design team level.

The result is far greater understanding and commitment than in traditional department-by-department design.

Section III.

The Six Most Common Causes of Failure

Poor organizational dynamics, not technical skill, dooms most Concurrent Engineering teams.

A basic rule:
"Design your team process before you begin to design your product!"

The following hurdles will challenge you and your Acme (your product line) design effort:

Inertia

"If it ain't broke, why fix it?" That's the attitude of many who will question the need to change a design system which has brought Acme to the top of our industry.

Acme's success over the past years is hard to dispute. The problem is that the market has changed dramatically. New conditions require new solutions.

But organizations resist change, especially when what has worked in the past has brought industry-wide success.

Many will challenge even the need to change the Acme design process. Change brings with it the need to learn new skills and work in a radically different way than in the past. Some may not want to make the personal investment in this kind of change.

Others will even see concurrent engineering as a threat to their job security. Done well, the process increases design efficiency. Design changes are fewer. Time wasted on the factory floor is less. Some support personnel may even feel threatened that they may lose their jobs.

Management must change its style. Managers must change from a traditional management posture to more of a leadership role. Functional departments play a different role than in the past.

These forces create a powerful force for staying with the status quo.

It is Acme management's task to recognize these forces and deal with them immediately. Design teams must also understand such resistance and be able to complete their task despite such hurdles.

Wrong Measurements

"Man performs as he or she is measured." Change measurements, and you will change human performance. Fail to change your measurements, and you will reward the status quo.

Using only traditional metrics, such as performance, direct cost, and schedule compliance, does not begin to focus the team's attention on life cycle Ilities such as serviceability, marketability and many others.

Wrong Players

"Nobody asked me for my input!"

Too many teams end up having the wrong people at the wrong time involved in the wrong way. Failure to involve all the right process owners early enough in order to understand the total business equation can get your design effort in serious trouble.

For example, manufacturing is involved by attending meetings but is not committed. Purchasing gets involved too late in the process to do any good.

Other team members attend meetings but play no meaningful pro-active role.

Multi-functional participation is needed for understanding *the enterprise-wide problem.*

Technical designers still solve technical problems. Manufacturing engineers still find factory-floor solutions. But all these tasks are done within the context of total success for Acme as a whole.

Wrong Tools

No single tool is enough to solve a design problem. Yet too often, design teams will use few, or even one tool, to solve their problem.

Too many fall for the "silver bullet" solution. Your initial task is to decide first the nature of the task and then select the right tool for the job.

Starting Late

Not enough design teams start their concurrent effort early enough, in the design concept stage.

These teams risk failure from the start by running into the "ugly baby" syndrome. This happens when the product performance designers come up with a design and then only later bring in the process owners to implement it.

When these latecomers begin to criticize the design for its manufacturability, serviceability or any number of other Ilities the result is inevitable: "Don't call my baby ugly!"

A basic rule: Gather your multi-functional team together at the early concept development stage. Avoid having one group creating a concept the rest of the team finds difficulty living with.

Not Enough Training, Coaching and Practice

When the U.S. Olympic Basketball team was selected in 1992, it represented the best sports talent America had to offer. This multifunctional team was a powerhouse of playing and coaching talent.

What did this all-star team do first? It launched itself into a rigorous schedule of training, coaching and practice. Nothing was taken for granted. They all recognized talent is nothing without team play, constantly reinforced by practice.

Yet countless concurrent engineering teams have set out with minimum, if any, training, weak coaching and absolutely no practice.

The result: Design efforts which never reach their full potential, or worse yet, fail to perform. Concurrent engineering teams must have a new game plan to guide them to success, a new method for overcoming the design problems of the past.

Avoid the danger of starting your team design without a new design methodology, strong managerial coaching and practice as a working team.

Section IV.

Common Sense Fundamentals You Must Know

Successful concurrent engineering comes from sticking to the basics.

The eleven common sense fundamentals described below may be easy to understand, but they can be extremely difficult to put into practice.

1. Focus on enterprise-wide success

Keep your eye on the ball. Solve your design trade-offs with the big picture view.

Focus on improving the entire Acme (your product line) design, not just optimizing your team's task.

2. Ask those who suffer from design flaws to help you correct them

Invite all process owners to help you write your real world design equation. Include all the (your product line) life cycle Ilities from marketability to serviceability.

Not only will the process owners educate you, they will have a greater understanding of the big picture and a greater dedication to solving it.

3. "A stitch in time saves nine"

Start early.

Form your complete team in the *design concept stage.* Every design effort, whether beginning with a clean sheet of paper or reworking an existing design starts with a concept stage.

The concept stage is when we make *strategic decisions* about performance requirements, manufacturing processes, and the nature of the competitive environment.

We also make basic assumptions about our company's capabilities and budget required to do the task.

Fielding your entire team early can surface problems early in the design cycle, avoiding loss of time, costly changes later.

4. Use new design methodology

Old methods yield old results. We must change *how* we design, the process by which we arrive at design decisions. The Strategic Design Method, currently being offered as part of our training effort, brings a new design approach which unifies a concurrent engineering effort from the start.

Not changing our design methodology means teams will design in the old, traditional manner.

5. Recruit a coaching staff

Ask functional line managers to serve on your coaching staff. Be proactive in seeking this help.

Functional managers generally see concurrent engineering as eroding their authority, dangerous for finding design solutions, and as taxing their already overloaded staff even more. The result: too many times, they resist Concurrent Engineering.

Make functional managers part of the solution, rather than part of the problem. Asking for the help of a multi-functional management task team brings experienced coaching talent to your design effort.

The support of functional managers can many times make or break a design team.

6. Understand the total design problem before you begin to solve it

Spend enough time understanding the total design problem before starting to solve it. All product designs are trade-offs between technical, organizational, and competitive requirements.

Make sure you are solving the right problem, at the right time, in the right way. Think design, not only engineering.

Engineering works at technical problems with usually well-defined requirements. But, design first asks "Do we have to solve this problem?" Don't begin solving your design equation before all life cycle issues, both business and technical, are understood by your entire design team.

7. Think of processes, not just product

The sum of the Acme (your product line) will be far more than the sum of its parts. It will be the sum of the life cycle processes required to design, manufacture, and support your product in the field.

Reduce the cost of the Acme (your product line) by eliminating both visible processes such as machining and assembling, and the thousands of hidden processes such as documenting, inspecting, re-working, and more.

Such hidden process steps can cost far more than the visible ones. Especially focus on design process steps. These cost not only dollars, but erode your most valuable asset-*time*.

8. Design your team process before your product

Decide how decisions are going to be made, how disputes are to be resolved, other team dynamics issues before you begin to work your technical problems.

Organizational inefficiency is the number one killer of concurrent engineering efforts.

9. Harness the power of team peer support

Concurrent engineering requires a total team effort to really work. Winning teams divide tasks with the primary goal being to minimize wasted meeting time.

For example, teams develop a system where one team member acts as a custodian for the interests of several other part-time members. This enables those members to skip meetings in which their participation would be minimal.

This kind of peer support maximizes team efficiency.

10. Keep management in the loop

Management dislikes surprises. Keep them informed about where you are going every step of the way.

First gain their understanding and agreement on how you and your team see the design challenge. Make sure both management and your team have a common starting point.

Don't begin to solve your design problem if management and your team do not have this mutual understanding.

Don't worry about briefing management too much. Remember that they are an invaluable source of experienced advice that can keep you out of trouble. Gain incremental agreement. Don't ask management to swallow your new design whole.

11. Measure...measure...measure

"Numbers talk, everything else walks!" That's how most senior managers think. When design concepts are presented without measurements attached, management immediately begins to lose their confidence in a design team.

But measurements available for use at the design concept stage are slim. That is why your design team must develop your own. The rule is "measure more, not less."

Everything is measureable. Develop measurements for each of your strategic design goals. Go well beyond the well-worn measurements of "performance, schedule and direct cost."

First identify the key Ilities you want imbedded in your design. Then develop ways of measuring how well your design concept is meeting them.

Think cause and effect. For example, measure serviceability if that is a key design goal. Brainstorm the key design causes of serviceability (the effect). These will include easy access to the service problem, readily available, off-the-shelf parts, low skill level for performing the service, and other causes.

Section V.

Your Seven Design Team Tasks and The Questions You Will Be Asked Most

This Section will help you through the seven key tasks needed for a successful design effort. Performing these tasks can spell the difference between success and failure for Acme and your design team.

Each section first gives a step-by-step explanation for each of the seven tasks. It is important to remember that a team's design task must drive its organizational response.

That is why no two concurrent engineering team organizations will ever be the same, even within Acme. Cookbook solutions are doomed to failure from the start.

Acme How To Questions

Following each of the seven tasks are questions actually asked by Acme people on how to "really make the process work." The answers provided for each will help guide you in your design improvement effort.

A caution: These answers are written to "jump start" your thought process. They are not application specific, ready to use "out of the box".

But they will give you 70-80% of the solution. Your task is then to fill in the blanks, shaping the rest of the answer to suit your individual circumstance.

The Seven Tasks

Here is a brief synopsis of the seven key tasks:

1. Empowering.

This is the management task of deciding who, when, and how concurrent engineering teams are set in motion. This includes the major team goals, budget, and overall design task boundaries.

Empowerment means giving the team permission or the capability to do what's right, within these overall management limits. Management's responsibility is to provide the needed time and dollars to make sure the team's design task can be accomplished in a timely manner.

2. Staffing.

This is the leadership task of deciding what skills are required for what period of time. The design task is first clearly defined by management, with functional departments providing the needed staff.

Teams are usually organized around a core of full- or nearly full-time members, with a support ring of part-time members.

3. Leading.

This is the task of motivating, guiding, and coaching both the core as well as the support ring.

Team leadership roles and responsibilities will vary with the design task. But in all cases the emphasis is on leading, rather than managing the team.

4. Organizing.

This is the collective team task of developing mission statements, agendas, reporting procedures, decision-making procedures and other human dynamics tools to assure the team is functioning well.

The responsibility for organizing efficiently must rest with the team. A fundamental of good team design is to "design your team human dynamics process first, design your product second."

5. Measuring.

This is the team task of setting design goals, within the limits of their management empowerment, and then developing meaningful measurements for tracking how well the team is meeting these goals.

New measurements must be added to the conventional ones of "schedule, performance and direct cost" in order to know if the team is really on track.

6. Motivating.

This is the Acme leadership task of providing both team and individual incentives to encourage the concurrent design process.

Both technical as well as team skill must be rewarded.

7. Leveraging.

This is the dual management and team responsibility for communicating lessons learned to others in Acme. This User's Guide, cross-training between teams, and other techniques help new teams avoid costly mistakes of the past.

Empowering

Empowering is the task of giving a design team the responsibility, training, and resources to get the job done.

Concurrent engineering efforts have little chance for success without solid, outspoken support by all senior management. Senior management's role is to provide broad guidelines and goals for design task teams.

It is the design task team's task to propose the design action plans, goals and on-going measurements to accomplish management's broad challenge.

This does not mean that senior management relinquishes total authority to the team. All task team decisions must be subject to management review.

Functional managers play the key roles of providing resources (team members qualified to do the work) and coaching. Their objective is to drive responsibility for making decisions down to the concurrent engineering team, not make decisions themselves.

Too often functional managers use an outdated "management-by-doing" style in this new concurrent environment, fearing failure by the team. The result is frustrated team members and mixed management signals.

This problem frequently occurs when senior executives have not clearly defined the functional manager's new role, provided him or her training in practicing this new role, and changed the management reward system to encourage this new coaching style.

Management Task Team Role

Creation of a top-level, cross-functional steering, or task team, can help facilitate the changeover to concurrent engineering Such a top level task team clearly signals that management is serious about accelerating the process.

The management task team usually operates under the charter of the company's overall quality improvement initiative.

Its goal is to integrate company management into the process on an enterprise-wide basis. The management task team can also begin to define the new roles of functional and project management, especially in the sometimes controversial areas of budget and authority.

The Management Task Team plays five major roles:

1. **Learning** how best to implement concurrent design in the Acme product development culture. This can come from benchmarking other companies, inputs from all levels at Acme, as well as from experiences with pilot design efforts.

2. **Guiding** the total implementation effort in its formative stages so that the process survives the rigors of inertia and internal turf problems. The Management Task Team can resolve the inevitable differences of opinion which can arise between design teams and functional departments.

3. **Coaching** design teams by providing experienced counsel, resources, and moral support, especially to pilot design team efforts. Making sure that all teams, as well as management, are adequately trained is a vital part of this coaching responsibility.

4. **Advising** senior management on the progress of the implementation effort and requesting appropriate enterprise-wide resources when needed. The Management Task Team directly interfaces with top company management to keep them up to date on progress.

5. **Measuring** bottom line results. The Management Task Team provides hard, quantifiable data on cost savings, cycle time reduction, and quality improvement, due to the concurrent design effort. These paybacks are measured beginning with the early design concept stage. The Task Team is also responsible for measuring the enterprise-wide implementation effort.

Design Team Formation

Concurrent design teams are formed to solve specific design tasks. These can range from designing a specific component or sub-assembly to conceptualizing an entire system.

The team is structured to meet the task. Since no two design tasks are ever identical, no two concurrent design teams are ever the same. Flexibility of response is the goal.

The general rule on team size is smaller is better. Should a design task prove too large or complex, it is sub-divided into smaller, more manageable tasks for other teams to manage. Expanding the team should be avoided.

The goal is to improve communication and total design ownership by keeping teams small.

New Versus Old Products

Concurrent engineering can be used for both new and existing products. Products already on the factory floor are being fine-tuned, sometimes with minimum tooling changes.

However, maximum leverage comes at the early design concept stage. This is where the design team can work the entire product as a *system*, and achieve major cost, quality, and cycle time breakthroughs.

Flexibility for improving existing products is sometimes limited due to existing investment and resource restrictions.

Design Team Sponsorship

"Sponsor" is the term used to identify the management person (sometimes a management task team as described above) designated to coach, motivate, guide and provide resources for the concurrent engineering team.

The design team reports directly to the Sponsor. The Sponsor is not a member of the team, nor is the leader of the team. He is the interface between the team and senior management.

The Sponsor's role is to act as the voice of senior management. He has the primary responsibility for facilitating the team's success, and usually reports to senior management on team progress, problems or roadblocks.

The Sponsor sets the major team goals for overall product objectives, timetable, budget and design constraints. This is done within the context of the company's overall business strategy.

The design team is then challenged to propose goals for their team within these broad limits. Relying on the design team to set these specific goals helps build greater understanding, goal ownership and faster time-to-completion.

All goals, however, are subject to the final approval of the Sponsor or senior management.

Team Empowerment

The design team has *collective ownership* of their total design. All individuals, whether full time or part time, are held accountable for the total effort, not just their contribution.

This principal of collective ownership is a powerful stimulus for reaching design compromises quickly. Collective ownership also helps to optimize a design for the entire company, and customer's, benefit.

The focal point of the team's effort is the "doing" of the design task. All members contribute to the effort, including the team leader.

While managers do serve on design teams, their role is usually not to manage but to do actual tasks. The continuing goal is to drive self-management to the lowest team level.

Organizational Types

Since no two design tasks are identical, each team will vary in its leadership style and organizational shape. Here are four of the most common types:

1. Advisory.

Functional departments called in from time-to-time to review design concepts developed by the product design staff. These reviews are usually called at the decision of the design project manager who has sole responsibility for all final decisions.

All the Ilities may not participate in the design evaluation process.

2. Focused.

Multi-functional team formed to review major product requirements. A project manager heads the team and retains primary decision-making authority.

Most times this is an intense burst of meetings held to resolve specific issues. Technical resources are matrixed.

Functional departments share members, subject to the constraints of their own department needs. Design staff owns the final design.

3. Formal.

Intact cross-functional team formed with formal core and part-time support members from functional departments. Members are assigned for the entire design project, with very few changes made.

All team members held accountable for success, failure of the entire design, not just their individual contribution. The leader is sometimes a manager, but the emphasis in decision-making is on consensus. The leader's goal is to build total team ownership.

4. Self-Managed.

Multi-functional team develops its own goals and measurements, subject to the approval of their Sponsor or management task team. Team members are all of roughly equal rank in the company hierarchy.

Members are asked to perform functions previously the responsibility of higher management. Their job description now includes both task identification and task completion. The team is asked what problems should be solved and when.

The total team owns the design. The team leader is a task doer. The leader's style is facilitative with the leadership role sometimes changing as the design project moves forward in time.

All members have the responsibility to challenge any action or decision they feel would adversely impact the product's success.

Team Authority

Teams provide periodic reports to their Sponsor, assuring management that they are on-track. This builds senior management confidence and helps avoid mis-communication with other project teams.

Types of decisions include:
- Definition of customer needs and requirements
- Conceptual design of the product, or system
- Engineering, development and test tasks
- Manufacturing process development
- Supplier sourcing policy
- Field service policy and procedures

Types of responsibilities include:
- Milestone scheduling
- Life cycle cost reduction
- Product quality
- Engineering change management
- Product development budget

Questions asked by Acme people about the empowerment process.

How does senior management empower the design team and still retain some influence on the project?

Senior management's job is to keep both design teams and the entire concurrent engineering process on track. Management does not relinquish its final authority on design decisions.

The best strategy is for senior management to set broad goals, while the design task team sets its own intermediate goals and measurements. It is then the responsibility of the team to gain management buy-in to these goals and measurements.

Shouldn't we all have the same definition for concurrent development? Is there such a thing as one, formal definition?

Avoid formal, precise definitions in favor of agreement on basic fundamentals. It is impossible to encompass all possible approaches in a few words.

Concurrent engineering is flexible, with each team deciding what approach is best for a specific design task. Hence there are many different combinations for making the process work.

Follow the fundamentals outlined in this section of your User's Guide. They allow you the freedom of designing the process to meet your particular need.

What is the definition of empowerment, as it applies to concurrent design?

Empowerment is management giving responsibility, time and resources to get things done to those who are best qualified for the task. It does not mean management is abdicating its responsibility or authority.

But empowerment is a two-way street. Design task teams must be willing to accept such empowerment and be able to deliver a design faster, with better quality and at lower total cost.

Who, when, and how are team leaders and members empowered with the authority to make decisions for their design project?

Management defines the broad boundaries at the start of the design effort. This is best done in writing.

The design team is then given an opportunity to completely understand these boundaries and buy into them. The objective is to build mutual understanding and agreement on goals between management and the team before beginning the design task.

Questions concerning resources, schedule, and budget should be surfaced at this early stage of the design effort.

What is functional management's new role?

Functional managers empower their employees to represent their department on the design team. The functional manager plays more of a coaching and training role in developing departmental human resources, rather than day-to-day management of the design process.

It is the employee's responsibility, however, to keep his functional manager completely informed about team progress and problems. This is especially important when these concern his manager's area of expertise.

The functional department continues to be primarily responsible for technical excellence.

How do we resolve the scope of authority question when functional management and project management issue guidelines that are opposed to one another?

Conflict between functional and project management is a common problem during the transition to concurrent design.

A Management Task Team can usually resolve most of these conflicts. One common technique is for the Task Team to identify and openly discuss potential points of conflict even before teams begin their design effort.

How do we get management to establish roles, responsibilities, procedures and guidelines in order to establish better team direction?

It is impossible for management to know all of the answers. The best technique is for management to first set broad guidelines and roles, and then rely on the design teams to help fill in the blanks.

This User's Guide is intended to help set these broad guidelines.

How do you get functional management to keep their influence on a design team in an advisory, not dictatorial role?

Functional management must first be trained in their new role, and then given the assurance by design teams that their functional design needs are being met.

Senior management must also re-define the functional manager's job. The performance review system must also be modified to reward this new kind of leadership behavior.

How do you integrate the design team review process with the existing corporate review cycle?

Effective concurrent engineering requires management interfacing with design teams beginning with the early conceptual stage. The objective is to have management play more of a *pro-active*, rather than review, role.

Reviews conducted late in the design cycle accomplish little, and can catch mistakes too late.

The Strategic Design Method integrates management experience with team effort, giving management a more pro-active, rather than a review, role.

Management can empower teams but this doesn't automatically mean teams will understand, accept and quickly act using this empowerment. What do you do when a team member doesn't accept the rules and conditions of empowerment?

Concurrent engineering requires that all players abide by the rules of the game. Team members who are unwilling to do so have no place on Acme design teams.

Staffing

Members on a concurrent engineering team are from all functional departments responsible for the life cycle of the product or service.

Membership can also include representation from suppliers, the product distribution network or even customers.

Core Team

Design teams usually consist of two rings. The inner, or core ring, consists of full-time or nearly full time members. The Core Team is the central driving force for the entire team.

While full-time membership on the Core Team is not essential, it usually results in better performance as it fosters the greatest intensity and dedication to the design task.

Core Team members are at roughly the same level in the company hierarchy. Team membership will vary from team to team. The team is "designed" to meet each specific design challenge.

Typical members can include:
- Product designers
- Systems engineers
- Process engineers
- Marketing representatives
- Field service engineers

Team member selection

There is no universal template for Core Team member selection as all design challenges differ. The kinds of technical skills represented may vary widely from team to team.

Besides representing their own functions, Core Team members can be expected to act as custodians for other part-time team participants.

For example, a design engineer may have the responsibility of representing the interests of a field service engineer who is not a member of the Core Team. The custodian makes sure the "voice" of the absent member is being heard. He also is responsible for briefing the absent member on team progress.

This custodianship technique builds confidence and trust between the Core Team and part-time support team members. It also encourages cross-training between both groups and a deeper understanding of each other's problems. Custodianship is an efficient way to save valuable meeting time.

Core Team Size

Fewer is better. Core Team size can be small with some teams having no more than four to eight members. Should the design task grow too large, the design task can be sub-divided into smaller tasks with smaller teams to solve them.

Communication problems can emerge when Core Teams begin to exceed ten members. Small team membership helps to overcome a major concurrent engineering challenge: poor communication.

Support Ring Membership

The Support Ring provides specialized support for the Core Team. Members serve on a part-time basis and are from major company Ility functions.

While the Support Ring may work for the team part-time, it still has an equal say in all major decisions. They are also held accountable for the entire design task success, not just their own contribution.

This recognizes Support Ring members must have full ownership in the design strategy if they are going to do their best in implementing that strategy.

Support Ring size will vary with the design task. Some members, such as marketing and sales, will play a major role early in the design. Others, such as tooling and manufacturing process development, will be more involved much later. As with the Core Team, the general rule is smaller is better.

Membership activity can shrink and grow as the design progresses. However, all team members are active during the early design concept stage which sets the scene for their implementation work later.

Suppliers and Customers

Successful concurrent engineering teams see suppliers as a valuable resource that must be involved in the design from the early requirements stage. Strategic partnerships can be formed with suppliers to better understand their needs and design for their requirements.

When confidentiality is an issue, the team can call on suppliers to play an educational role, briefing the team on the latest technology without involving the supplier directly in the design task.

Customer participation can range from the team meeting with focus customer groups to one-on-one meetings between customer engineers and the team. The marketing and sales team still play the important role of maintaining and managing customer relationships, but the design team has a clearer picture of customer needs.

Duration of Membership

Successful teams avoid changing membership. Members should stay the length of the design project. This builds commitment to the design. It also builds confidence and trust among the membership.

For example, when a new replaces an old member, the new member may not buy-in to all of the design decisions made previously.

Members usually remain with the team until the design is launched. However, the goal is to have all team members having a sense of ownership of the design throughout its entire life cycle.

Team Member Qualities

All members require both technical and interpersonal skills to be successful. Core Team members must be especially self-motivated, possess a sense of urgency, and be dedicated to the company's goals.

Team members must clearly understand their work load will increase, not decrease, with their participation on the team. It is up to the individual team member to maximize his efficiency so that all his tasks, both for his functional department and for his team, are completed on time and with excellence.

The task of balancing both the team's needs and his department's needs is primarily the individual team member's responsibility, not his manager's task.

Membership Recruitment

It is normally the team leader's responsibility, working with the advice and concurrence of his Sponsor, to lead the Core Team membership selection.

For pilot team efforts, the Management Task Team sometimes can play a role in member selection. But in both cases, functional managers must have the final authority for whether an individual will be a member of the team.

This places the responsibility for human resource development squarely on the shoulders of the functional manager. It is the functional manager who must play the key roles of coaching, training, and developing team members.

Team leaders can negotiate with functional departments for both Core and Support Team members. The leader does this by clearly identifying the skills and time required for team participation. He then sets up a reporting procedure to keep the functional manager informed once his team is underway.

Such a negotiated agreement builds a good working relationship between the design team leader and the functional manager from the start.

Membership Responsibilities

Core Team members, in most cases, do not serve on multiple teams. This usually dilutes the intensity of their effort.

Support Team members, however, do serve on multiple teams. The responsibility for how much time is spent on each is usually resolved by the Support Team member himself. The team member's manager sets the broad time guidelines with the individual responsible for when and how his time is to be spent.

Support Team members who serve on multiple teams yield such positive benefits as:

- Cross-pollination of design ideas
- Company-wide design consistency
- Improved technical communication
- Cross-training among technical disciplines

Core Team members act as custodians for Support Team member interests. The constant goal is to reduce the amount of time Support Team members must spend in meetings. The Custodian's responsibilities include:

- Keeping the Support Ring member up-to-date
- Taking his point of view in discussions
- Making sure he attends meetings where his key interests are at stake.

Time Allocation

Time required for a Support Ring member can range from 10% to 100% of his personal schedule, depending on design development stage. The objective is always efficient use of time — only having the Support Ring member on hand when he is really needed.

Support Ring members are encouraged to share their technical expertise with (cross-train) Core Team members in order to expand the team's overall technical competency.

Membership Changes

Membership consistency must be the goal. Only in extreme cases should membership of the Core Team be changed. The reason is that team commitment to a common design strategy degrades rapidly with frequent membership changes.

Another problem is that new team members may not buy-in to decisions made previous to them joining the team.

Decision-Making Responsibility

Both Core Team and Support Team members must share equally in major decision-making. This builds better understanding and stronger commitment to implementing design decisions. The design process should not move forward until this buy-in is reached.

All team members must have the full confidence of their functional management to make such decisions. This places the responsibility for selecting capable team members squarely on the shoulders of functional management. Excessive sideline calls must be avoided.

Questions asked by Acme people about the team staffing process.

Who selects team members? How is this selection best done?

Team selection is a joint effort of the Sponsor, team leader, and functional department managers.

The team leader and Sponsor first define their resource needs in terms of "talent and time" and then "negotiate" with functional departments for the people needed.

What can motivate functional management to buy into risk sharing? To take ownership in multi-functional team decisions?

What is the responsibility of the design team's "second ring" to the total design effort?

How do we make sure our team has the right people on the right teams with the right skills?

What training should be developed for Acme design teams?

Our resources at Acme are stretched thin. One specialist may have to be divided between several teams. Who decides how one of these second ring specialists should be spending his/her time between teams?

To what extent should marketing and sales be allowed to change design requirements? Such changes can significantly impact both schedule and cost.

What is the role of Acme suppliers and customers on these teams?

Leading

Leadership is the task of motivating, guiding and coaching both the Core Team and the Support Team.

Leadership styles will vary widely from team to team, depending both on the design task and the personality of the leader. There is no one right leadership style.

The leader is also a doer on a design task team. He completes design assignments, reports back to the team's sponsor as well as his own functional department management.

Managers are not usually leaders of task teams. The goal is to build team self-management. Team members usually will accept a greater degree of responsibility for their performance when management is external to the team process.

Leadership Selection

The Sponsor, or Management Task Team in the case of a pilot concurrent design effort, usually selects the team leader. This is done with the input of other functional department managers.

The leader, in turn, then works with the Sponsor on defining the skills required for staffing the team. This transfers the primary responsibility for team selection to the team leader.

Asking team members to choose their own leaders usually does not work well in the intensity of a product design effort. The success of a design team will usually have a major impact on the success of the entire company.

Teams without total management confidence in their leadership either have continual management help or sometimes very short life spans.

Team Skills Required

The Team Leader must have three key skills:
- Leadership Skill
- Technical Skill
- Political Skill

Leadership skill is the ability to instill a sense of common commitment to the design task throughout the product development effort. He must be able to motivate, coach and guide his team. The leader must be a people person, preferably with previous experience or leadership training.

Technical skill is the ability to understand all technical issues related to solving the design task. The leader does not need to be the most technically skilled individual on the team.

Political skill is the ability to build support for his team effort throughout the company. The concurrent design process sometimes runs counter to traditional company practices, crossing boundaries or turf considered sacred ground by some managers.

The effective leader must know how to navigate in these sometimes hostile waters. He must be familiar with his company's culture and be able to build cross-company departmental support for his design team.

Leadership Qualities

Leadership capability should be ranked higher than technical capability in the selection process. The best leader is one who has a proven track record in the tasks of inspiring, coaching, and motivating a team.

When previous experience is lacking, leaders should be trained in their new role before launching the team effort. Leadership skills are very difficult to learn on the job, especially during the intensity of a design effort.

Leadership Rank

The leader selected should be of roughly equal rank to his fellow team members. This helps build team unity and peer support. The goal is always to have equal responsibility and ownership of the team design task.

Appointing an individual of higher rank can erode the sense of common team responsibility for their actions.

Leadership Roles

In keeping with the concept of team and individual self-management, the leader plays a more facilitative, rather than managerial, role. His objective is to have the team reach consensus decisions, thus building greater understanding and willingness to implement design decisions.

The leader realizes that commitment to group success is greatest when all team members own the decision. Depending on the design task and previous team agreement, however, the leader may mandate decisions. But this must be done with the team fully understanding why the decision was made and what their role is in carrying it out.

The leader plays the dual role of both doing and leading. He is an active member of the team, completing design tasks as are his fellow members.

Only in extreme cases should a team's leadership be changed. Such techniques as rotating the leaderships as the nature of the design task changes are usually disruptive. Replacing a team leader in the mid-stream of a design effort can destroy team momentum as the leader brings himself up to speed, possibly create distrust and even result in team factions.

Questions asked by Acme people about team leadership process.

Who selects team leaders? What skills does the leader need?

In many cases, project and functional management don't see "eye to eye" on a particular decision. Who do we satisfy?

How do you encourage Acme functional managers to "buy into" project goals?

What kind of program should be put in place for senior management to understand, lead and support concurrent engineering activity?

How do we build better understanding between disciplines serving on the design team?

How can we build better team concepts and teamwork?

How does the team leader handle strong personalities on a design team?

What can be done when a concurrent engineering leader, or team members, try to overrule functional department specialists?
How can we make sure the "voice of functional management" is being heard?

Organizing

The first rule of any team design effort is:

Design your team organization first, well before starting on your product design.

Too many design teams fail because they spend little, or no time, on building a strong organizational structure.

Design team organization is the collective task of developing roles, mission statements, agendas, reporting procedures, decision-making systems and other human dynamics tools to help a team operate smoothly.

Why Organization is Important

Most design efforts flounder because of poor team dynamics, rather than a lack of technical skills. Good organization assures all team members and their functional departments are "in tune." The goal is to keep misunderstanding at a minimum.

When To Begin

Designing how the team will be organized is the first step in any design effort. The task of designing the product is the second step. All organizational decisions should be discussed and agreed to by the entire team long before the design effort starts.

One effective technique is to write a Team Mission Statement outlining the overall task and outlining team member duties. Issues covered should include:

- Roles: Who does what
- Decision-making: Who, When and How
- Reporting: To Whom, When and How

Team Location

Full-time team co-location improves team communication, but is a double-edged sword. Co-location can:

- Strain company space and equipment budgets
- Detach team members from their functional support group
- Result in a company-within-a-company feeling on the part of non team members

Questions asked by Acme people about how to organize concurrent design teams.

If customer satisfaction is the ultimate criterion, how is this introduced into the team design process?

What can be done to assure all design team members are aware of all design requirements up front?

How do we, as a Acme design team, convince management that there is need for additional resources, i.e., facilities and personnel?

How is the rest of Acme company management kept up to speed on team progress?

Should we co-locate all design teams?

How large should the task of each design team be?

How do we at Acme make sure separate design teams are integrated?

How can core team members keep second ring specialists informed?

How can we make sure everything is done on time?

How do we know when to freeze a design?

Measuring

Measurement is the collective team task of making sure the effort to reach the design goals are on track.

The team has the dual task of setting product development goals, within the limits of their empowerment, as well as developing measurements for those goals.

Performance Assessment

Functional departments still retain the responsibility for measuring the effectiveness of their team members. But major performance assessments, especially for Core Team members, are conducted with the input of the team leader.

Progress Reviews

Progress reviews will vary depending on the dimension and intensity of the design task. It is the task of the design team to propose to management, or the team sponsor, when and how frequently these reviews will take place.

Questions asked by Acme people about the design team measurement process.

How do you assess the effectiveness of our concurrent engineering activity? How do we at Acme measure progress?

Business issues are every bit as important as technical ones. How do we make sure both are being considered in a design trade-off?

What do we do when upper management becomes too worried that they see no results?

What criteria can be established for reviewing overhead hidden cost during the design stage? Specific cost information is hard to come by in the early design stage.

Life cycle cost is now a major issue at Acme. How do you ingrain life cycle costs into the minds of the design team members?

How can you establish quantified goals for cost elimination, both at the team level and the overall project level?

How do you get cost data for hidden costs?

What do we as managers do if a team is not meeting its goals? How do we go about modifying the process on the team to help it achieve its goals?

Given the importance of having one, unified, shared goal by the entire team, what should we do when one discipline, engineering for example, overly directs the goal setting process?

Motivating

Motivating is management's task of providing team, as well as individual, incentives for excellence in both technical as well as interpersonal skills.

It is extremely important for both the company, team sponsor, and design team leader to reach concurrence on goals prior to beginning the design effort. This is the primary reason why a Strategic Design Brief should be completed at the beginning of the team's effort.

Financially rewarding the team as a unit has proven both difficult and can be counter productive. A very powerful reward is team recognition, both within the company and outside. For example, one successful technique used is to publicize the success of a new product, as well as the team responsible for it, in the trade press.

Recognition rewards have a far longer lasting and wider effect than financial rewards. Such rewards clearly show what kind of individual and team performance the company considers essential for its success. Individual rewards should be made after the team task is completed, or clearly separate from the team performance.

Questions asked by Acme people about how to motivate design teams.

How do I support project goals when my personal evaluation is by functional management and the functional goals are different from the project goals?

How do you deal with old-style managers who honestly do not see themselves as obstacles to concurrent development?

Why, and how, do team members retain ties to functional department management?

How do you motivate team members for input into a conceptual design?

Accepting the fact that senior management has empowered our design teams, how do you get the teams to accept coaching?

How do we make teamwork from top to bottom seamless?

How do we establish a reward system for multi-functional teams?

What reward systems seem to work best for this process?

Leveraging

Leveraging is the task of putting lessons learned to work on future concurrent engineering efforts. This is a joint management and team responsibility.

Should the same successful team be used on a new design task? Experience shows this should be avoided. The winning magic and intensity of the second effort never seems to match the first.

Appointing team members from successful design efforts to new teams is the most effective way to communicate lessons learned. It is one of the most believable as well, since we tend to trust more those who have actually been part of the process.

Constantly updating this User's Guide to include results of successful design efforts is a very effective way to capture lessons learned.

Questions asked by Acme people about how to learn from the success, and failures, of Acme design teams.

How do we at Acme put in place a review process so that we can take advantage of lessons learned?

Should a successful design team be kept intact and used for a new design challenge?

Section VI.

Acme Lessons Learned

(Include in this section examples of your previous design team successes. They need not even have been called concurrent engineering efforts. The best format is a before and after matrix showing all the design goals. Easy-to-understand three dimensional product drawings should accompany the data.)

Addendum

The Most Asked Questions About The Strategic Design Method

What is Strategic Design?

Strategic Design is a *methodology* for accelerating the concurrent engineering process.

How effective is Strategic Design?

Strategic Design is now being used by concurrent engineering teams to reduce costs by 30%, or more, improve quality to Six Sigma levels, and reduce design time by half.

How is it different from Design of Experiments (DOE)? Quality Function Deployment (QFD)? Other design tools?

Strategic Design is a method for integrating these tools, helping them work even better. Strategic Design helps your design team decide which of these tools should be used and when.

Who should use Strategic Design?

Strategic Design is used by the entire multi-functional design team. It requires the participation of the entire team to make it effective.

When should Strategic Design be used?

Strategic Design is used at the start of the concurrent engineering process. Strategic Design gets the entire design team launched up front and right!

Why is it important to use Strategic Design?

Strategic Design integrates the efforts of all cross-functional team members. It requires all team members to play a *pro-active role* in design improvement. It does away with the traditional review mentality of traditional design.

How do we know Strategic Design is successful?

All Strategic Design tools come with metrics, or *measurements*, to tell you how much you have improved your design.

Where can Strategic Design be used?

Strategic Design can be used for any product or process. Today it is used in all industries, from electronics to automotive, and to improve a wide range of products, from microchips to potato chips.

What will Strategic Design help us improve?

Strategic Design reduces total life cycle cost, improves quality to Six Sigma levels, and shortens both design and manufacturing cycle time.

How does Strategic Design work?

Strategic Design enables your design team to see their product, or service, as a *total system*. It shows your design team how to eliminate unneeded tasks, or *processes,* during your product's entire life cycle.

How is Strategic Design different from Design for Manufacturability, Design for Quality, other "Design For" tools?

Strategic Design enables you to address all these Ilities *concurrently*. It *helps you rank these* in importance, helping you to *focus on the most important Ilities.*

What kind of costs can we reduce with Strategic Design?

All costs, especially hidden ones like overhead and burden. These *hidden costs* now account for more than 30% of all product costs. Most teams do not include these kinds of costs in their design equations, yet they can be your company's biggest cost headache.

Who developed Strategic Design?

Strategic Design was developed by Bart Huthwaite, Sr., founder of the Institute For Competitive Design, Rochester, Michigan. Huthwaite is a pioneer in the "Design for Excellence" field. Strategic Design is based on ten years of research and hands-on experience in how to make concurrent engineering work more efficiently.

How difficult is it to learn Strategic Design?

Strategic Design does not require any technical expertise or pre-training. Design teams can begin using the methodology within hours to improve their own designs.

What other companies are now using Strategic Design?

Motorola, Lockheed, Ford Motor, and more than 300 other industry leaders, both large and small.

Who teaches Strategic Design?

Strategic Design is *easily taught* by an in-house facilitator or team leader. It does not require outside consultants or experts.

Products and Services

The Institute For Competitive Design
134 W. University Dr.
Rochester, Michigan 48307

Phone: 313-656-2195
Fax: 313-656-2365

Public Workshops

These workshops help facilitators, team leaders, managers, and design team members work better, more efficiently. Attendees take home design methodology tools for reducing cost, improving quality and reducing cycle time. Workshops are sponsored with DESIGN NEWS, SDRC, and other leading design organizations with Bart Huthwaite, Sr., ICD Founder/Director, presenting all material. One and three-day formats are offered throughout the year. ICD also offers public workshops to expose you to the power of Strategic Design. These workshops are located in convenient locations throughout the U.S. Call ICD for dates and locations.

On-Site Services

All services provided at your organization by Bart Huthwaite, Sr., ICD Founder/Director. Contact ICD for details.

Needs Assessment One-day review of your concurrent engineering effort, followed by "no holds barred' presentation to your senior executives on how your company compares to others.

Strategic Design Workshop One, two or three-day on-site workshops for 25-30 participants. Your employees design on all days, actually re-designing one of your own products by the second day. Bart Huthwaite has trained over 200,000 people at more than 300 leading companies over the past decade. A Strategic Design workshop is excellent for launching concurrent engineering design teams. All workshops are customized for your product and industry. Contact ICD for training agendas and references.

Design Team Coaching Bart Huthwaite coaches your concurrent engineering design team. This coaching usually requires four days and uses the Strategic Design Method.

Off-Site Services

Off-Site services are designed to help facilitators get up and running quickly at minimum cost. Bart Huthwaite, Sr. consults by phone, fax, computer modem reviewing implementation strategies, coaching facilitators on User's Guides, training tools, and other concurrent engineering techniques.

Videotape Training

This 12-part concurrent engineering training series enables facilitators to present their own on-site training. Training can be customized to your company's product or industry. All six hours of videotape were professionally produced at General Motors Institute, using a live workshop audience. Training series includes 150-page "Concurrent Engineering Handbook" for use during workshop and as a reference later. Contact ICD for complete details, and demonstration tapes.

Divisional licenses also available with right to reproduce tapes, customize and print your own Handbooks.

Facilitator Software Kits

These Microsoft-based products help concurrent engineering facilitators get up and running quickly at minimum cost.

"Concurrent Engineering User's Guide" Software, templates, techniques, step-by-step instruction in how to write your own customized "User's Guide" for concurrent engineering teams.

"Concurrent Engineering Benchmarking Template" Software, templates, techniques, step-by-step instruction in how to design your own Malcom-Baldrige-type measurement tool. Enable you to baseline where your company is at, provide management with quantitative measurements of progress.